CHILDCRAFT
THE HOW AND WHY LIBRARY

SEE THE WORLD

D1540721

WORLD
BOOK

a Scott Fetzer company
Chicago
www.worldbookonline.com

Childcraft—The How and Why Library
2009 revised printing

CHILDCRAFT, CHILDCRAFT—THE HOW AND WHY LIBRARY, HOW AND WHY, WORLD BOOK and the GLOBE DEVICE are registered trademarks or trademarks of World Book, Inc.

World Book, Inc.
233 N. Michigan Avenue
Chicago, IL 60601

The Library of Congress has cataloged a previous edition of this title as follows:

Childcraft: the how and why library.
   v. cm.
  Summary: Presents illustrated articles, stories, and poems, grouped thematically in fifteen volumes.
  Includes bibliographical references and indexes.
  Contents: v. 1. Poems and rhymes -- v. 2. Once upon a time -- v. 3. Art around us -- v. 4. The world of animals -- v. 5 The world of plants -- v. 6. Our earth -- v. 7. The universe -- v. 8. How does it happen? -- v. 9. How things work -- v. 10. Shapes and numbers -- v. 11. About you -- v. 12. Who we are -- v. 13. See the world -- v. 14. Celebrate! -- v. 15. Guide and index.
  ISBN 0-7166-2203-3 (set)
  1. Children's encyclopedias and dictionaries.
  [1. Encyclopedias and dictionaries.]
  I. Title: Childcraft. II. World Book, Inc.
  AG6 .C48 2004
  031--dc21   2003008722

This printing:
ISBN 978-0-7166-2235-2 (set)
ISBN 978-0-7166-2248-2 (Volume 13, See the World)

Printed in China
5 6 7 8 9 13 12 11 10 09

Acknowledgments
de la Mare, Walter: "Somewhere" (first verse) from *The Complete Poems of Walter de la Mare.* © 1969 (USA: 1970). By permission of the Literary Trustees of Walter de la Mare and the Society of Authors as their representatives.

Silverstein, Shel: "Surprise" from *A Light in the Attic* by Shel Silverstein. Copyright © 1981 by Evil Eye Music, Inc. By permission of HarperCollins Publishers and Edite Kroll Literary Agency, Inc.

For information on other World Book publications, visit our Web site at **http://www.worldbookonline.com** or call **1-800 WORLDBK (967-5325)**. For information on sales to schools and libraries, call **1-800-975-3250 (United States)** or **1-800-837-5365 (Canada)**.

Contents

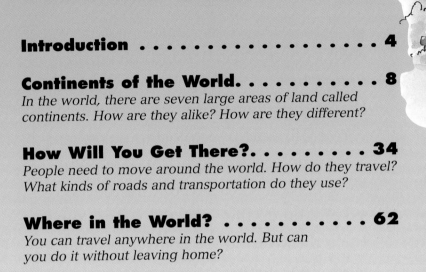

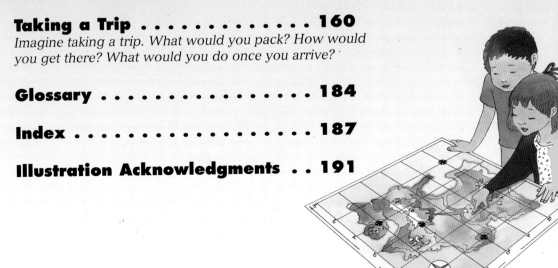

Introduction

Let's go on a trip around the world today! Just open the pages of *See the World,* and your journey will begin.

You will start by exploring the seven huge land areas called continents. But were there always seven? Are they all alike? And do they stay the same? You'll enjoy discovering the answers in the pages that follow.

You will also find out the many ways that people travel from place to place—for example, in cars and buses on roads, in boats across water, and in airplanes

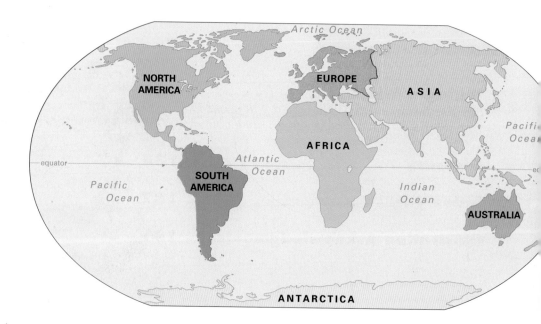

through the sky. But other ways of traveling are far less common. Some people travel on camels across the sand. Others use dogsleds to cover the distance on snow and ice.

There are lots of famous places to visit throughout the world, including castles, skyscrapers, towers, bridges, and monuments. Some of the world's most amazing structures were built long ago, such as the Great Pyramid of Giza in Egypt and the Great Wall of China.

If all this armchair travel has made you want to get out there and see the world in person, the book can help more. You will learn how maps help you find your way around, and then you can start planning your own trip!

There are many features in this book to help you find your way through it. The boxes marked **Know It All!** have fun-filled facts. You can amaze your friends with what you learn!

This book also has many activities that you can do at home. Look for the words **Try This!** over a colored ball. The activity that follows offers a hands-on

Know It All! boxes have fun-filled facts.

Each activity has a number. The higher the number, the more adult help you may need.

An activity that has this colorful border is a little more complex than one without the border.

way to learn more about the world. For example, you can make your own map or compass.

Each activity has a number in its colored ball. Activities with a 1 in a green ball are simplest to do. Those with a 2 inside a yellow ball may require a little adult help with tasks such as cutting or measuring. Activities with a 3 inside a red ball may need more adult help.

A Try This! activity that has a colorful border around its entire page is a little more complex or requires a few more materials. Take a moment to review the list of materials needed and to read through the step-by-step instructions before you begin.

As you read this book, you will see that some words are printed in bold type, **like this.** These are words that might be new to you. You can find the meanings and pronunciations of these words in the **Glossary** at the back of the book. Turn to the **Index** to look up page numbers of subjects that interest you the most.

If you enjoy learning about places around the world, find out more in other resources, such as those listed below. Check them out at a bookstore or at your library.

Alice Ramsey's Grand Adventure, by Don Brown, 1997. *This book describes the adventures of Alice as she takes a car trip from New York and San Francisco in 1909, becoming the first woman to drive across the United States.*

Amelia Hits the Road, by Marissa Moss, 1999. *Amelia writes about her family's road trip to California and some of the national parks they see on the way.*

Boats Afloat, by Shelley Rotner, 1998. *This book is filled with photos of all kinds of boats.*

Children Just Like Me: A Unique Celebration of Children Around the World, by Barnabas and Anabel Kindersley, 1995. *Beautiful photographs in this book show the clothing, housing, work, and play of children from all parts of the world.*

Houses, by Gallimard Jeunesse and Claude Delafosse, 1998. *In this book you will see the different kinds of houses in which people from around the world live.*

How to Make an Apple Pie and See the World, by Marjorie Priceman, 1996. *Take a trip around the world to gather the ingredients to make an apple pie.*

Illustrated Atlas by World Book, Inc., 2003. *Visit all the regions of the world. Meet the people and see what the land, animals, and plants are like around the world in this well-illustrated, oversized atlas.*

Market, by Ted Lewin, 2000. *Find out what people grow, catch, or make as you visit markets around the world.*

Roundabouts: Our Globe, Our World, by Kate Petty and Jakki Wood, 2000. *Harry finds out about maps, globes, the equator, continents, and much more as he takes a trip with his dog, Ralph, in a hot-air balloon.*

World Adventure, by World Book, Inc., 2000. *Imagine if you and three of your friends could take a trip around the world in a year. What would you see and do? Find out what these four characters did by reading their group journal, postcards, guidebook, newspaper clippings, snapshots, and more!*

Continents of the World

The earth has seven huge land areas called continents. Some are connected to each other. Others are completely surrounded by water. These chunks of land are so large that some may have snowy mountains on one part and steamy forests on another. They may have dozens of countries or just one. What are the names of these seven continents, and how is each one special? Which one is the largest? Which one has the most people? Read on to find out!

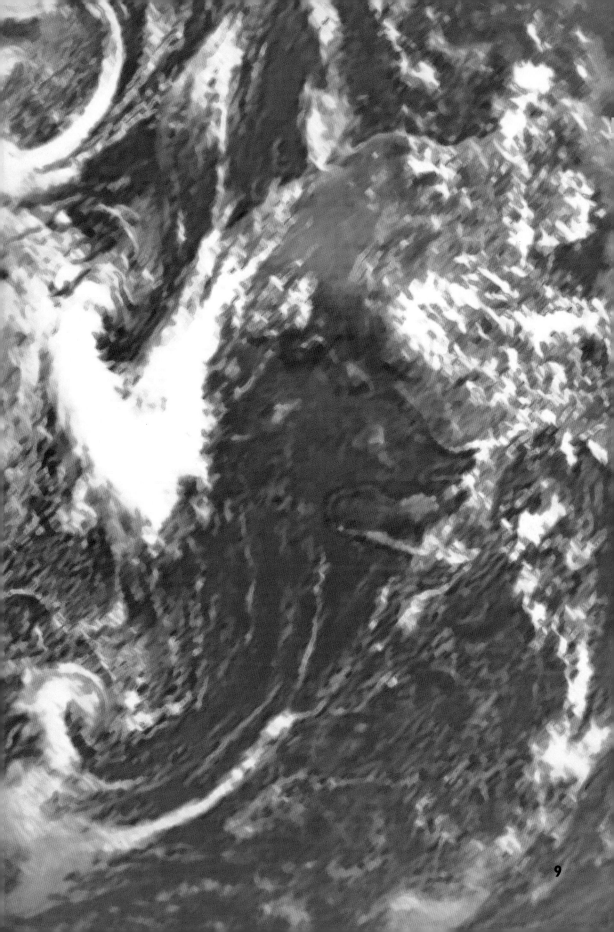

9

What Are the Seven Continents?

The seven **continents** are Africa, Antarctica, Asia, Australia, Europe, North America, and South America. Australia is an island, a piece of land totally surrounded by water. But it is such a huge island that it is also a continent. Other continents, such as Europe and North America, have islands that are considered a part of them. There are also thousands of smaller islands, such as a group of islands called the Pacific Islands, that are not counted as part of the continents. Europe and Asia are joined on one side, but they are thought of as two continents.

This map of the world shows where the seven continents are. You can tell a lot about the continents by studying the map. For example, if you look closely, you will see that each continent has a different shape. Use tracing paper to trace the shape of each continent.

equ

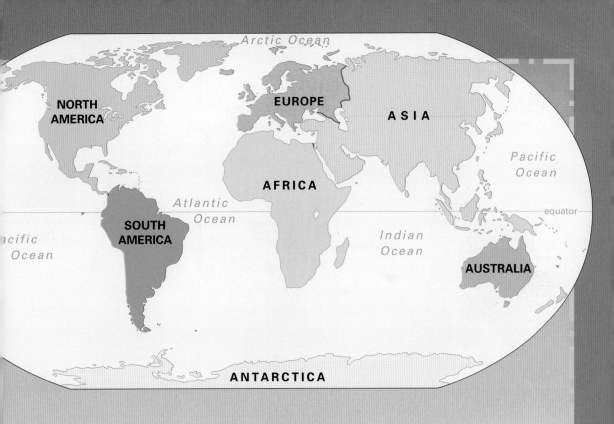

NORTH AMERICA

EUROPE

ASIA

Pacific Ocean

AFRICA

Atlantic Ocean

equator

SOUTH AMERICA

Pacific Ocean

Indian Ocean

AUSTRALIA

ANTARCTICA

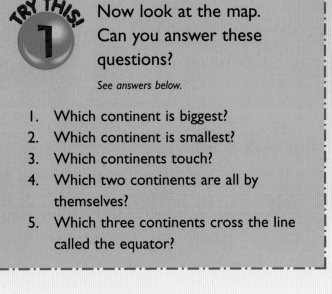

TRY THIS!

1

Now look at the map. Can you answer these questions?

See answers below.

1. Which continent is biggest?
2. Which continent is smallest?
3. Which continents touch?
4. Which two continents are all by themselves?
5. Which three continents cross the line called the equator?

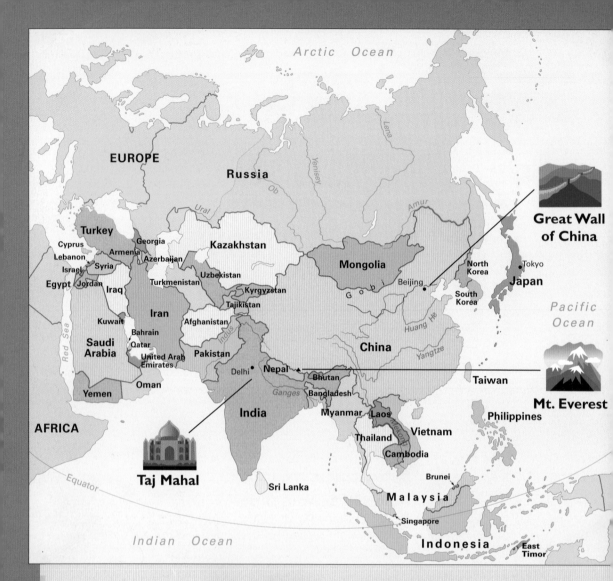

Map of Asia showing countries and features including Arctic Ocean, Europe, Russia, Turkey, Cyprus, Lebanon, Israel, Egypt, Jordan, Syria, Iraq, Georgia, Armenia, Azerbaijan, Kazakhstan, Turkmenistan, Uzbekistan, Kyrgyzstan, Tajikistan, Iran, Afghanistan, Kuwait, Bahrain, Qatar, Saudi Arabia, United Arab Emirates, Pakistan, Oman, Yemen, Mongolia, Beijing, North Korea, South Korea, Japan, Tokyo, China, Taiwan, Delhi, Nepal, Bhutan, Bangladesh, India, Myanmar, Laos, Thailand, Vietnam, Cambodia, Philippines, Brunei, Malaysia, Singapore, Sri Lanka, Indonesia, East Timor. Landmarks: Great Wall of China, Mt. Everest, Taj Mahal. Oceans: Pacific Ocean, Indian Ocean. Rivers: Lena, Yenisey, Ob, Ural, Amur, Huang He, Yangtze, Indus, Ganges, Mekong. Gobi desert, Red Sea, Equator. AFRICA.

Asia

Asia is the largest continent by far. It has more land and more people than any other continent. It is so big that Australia and North America could fit inside it. Asia and Europe are joined along one side.

Asia has some of the world's highest mountains, largest deserts and **plains**, and thickest jungles. There are cold deserts in central and northern Asia, hot deserts in the southwest, and steamy tropics in the southeast. Many Asians live in crowded cities, such as Tokyo in Japan, Delhi in India, and Beijing in China. But there are also many places in Asia where very few people live.

There are 50 countries in Asia. Two of the world's largest countries, Russia and China, are in Asia. In fact, Russia is so big that it lies on two continents. Part of it is in Europe and part of it is in Asia.

Visitors to Asia often visit the Great Wall of China. It was built more than 1,000 years ago and stretches thousands of miles long across north-central China. Many mountain climbers are drawn to Asia's Mount Everest, the highest peak in the world.

Highest mountain:
Mount Everest,
29,028 feet
(8,848 meters)
Longest river:
Yangtze (yahng dzuh),
3,915 miles
(6,300 kilometers)
Largest desert:
Gobi (GOH bee),
500,000 square miles (1,300,000 square kilometers)

The Taj Mahal is a famous tomb in India. An Indian shah, or king, built it for his wife in the 1600's.

13

Africa

Africa is the second largest continent. Steamy tropical rain forests cover parts of western and central Africa. The Sahara Desert stretches across most of the northern part. The longest freshwater

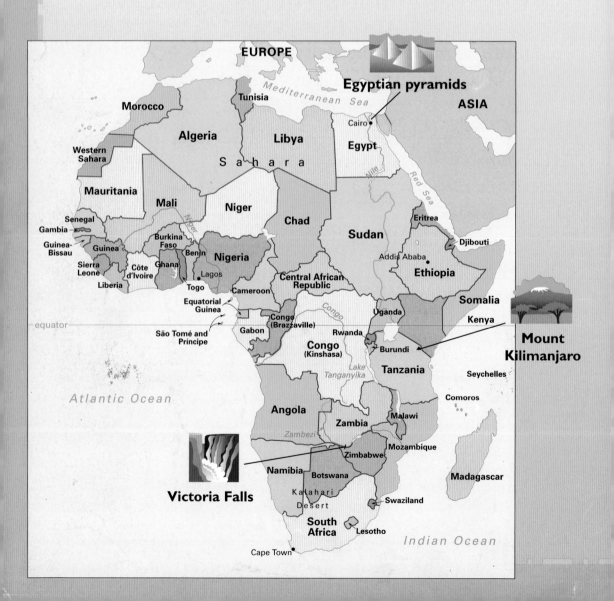

EUROPE

Egyptian pyramids

ASIA

Tunisia

Mediterranean Sea

Morocco

Algeria

Libya

Egypt

Cairo

Western Sahara

S a h a r a

Nile

Red Sea

Mauritania

Mali

Niger

Chad

Sudan

Eritrea

Senegal

Niger

Djibouti

Gambia

Burkina Faso

Addis Ababa

Guinea-Bissau

Guinea

Benin

Nigeria

Ethiopia

Sierra Leone

Côte d'Ivoire

Ghana

Lagos

Liberia

Togo

Cameroon

Central African Republic

Somalia

Equatorial Guinea

Congo

Uganda

Kenya

equator

São Tomé and Príncipe

Gabon

Congo (Brazzaville)

Rwanda

Mount Kilimanjaro

Congo (Kinshasa)

Burundi

Lake Tanganyika

Tanzania

Seychelles

Atlantic Ocean

Comoros

Angola

Zambia

Malawi

Mozambique

Zambezi

Victoria Falls

Zimbabwe

Namibia

Botswana

Madagascar

Kalahari Desert

Swaziland

South Africa

Lesotho

Indian Ocean

Cape Town

These school children visit the pyramids in Giza, Egypt, a popular spot for tourists.

lake in the world, Lake Tanganyika (TANG guhn YEE kuh), lies in eastern Africa.

A sea separates most of Africa and Asia, but in one place the two continents meet.

Africa has 53 countries. Its largest country is Sudan. The smallest is Seychelles (say SHEHL). Most Africans live in rural areas, but some live in cities such as Addis Ababa in Ethiopia, Cape Town in South Africa, and Lagos in Nigeria.

Many people travel to Africa to study its wild animals, visit such ancient sites as the pyramids of Egypt, or see such natural wonders as Victoria Falls and Kilimanjaro, a towering volcano that is no longer active.

Highest mountain: *Kilimanjaro*, 19,340 feet (5,895 meters)
Longest river: *Nile*, 4,145 miles (6,671 kilometers)
Largest desert: *Sahara*, 3 1/2 million square miles (9 million square kilometers)

15

North America

North America is the third largest continent. It has fewer people than Europe, Asia, or Africa. The northern part of the continent is near the North Pole. The southern part is connected to South America by a narrow strip of land. The north has icy plains. The south has sunny beaches.

Bikers enjoy the view at Acadia National Park, Maine.

North America includes magnificent mountain peaks, sandy deserts, flat grasslands, and thick forests.

North America has 23 countries. Canada is the biggest, but the United States has the most people. Major North American cities include Calgary, Montreal, and Toronto, in Canada; Chicago, Los Angeles, and New York, in the United States; Havana, in Cuba; and Mexico City, in Mexico.

ASIA

North Pole

Greenland (Denmark)

United States

Mount McKinley ▲

Yukon

Mackenzie

Canada

CN Tower

Vancouver

Calgary

Atlantic Ocean

Pacific Ocean

Montreal

Missouri

Chicago

Toronto

New York City

Colorado

Mississippi

Los Angeles

United States

Dallas

Sonoran Desert

Grand Canyon

Mexico

Statue of Liberty

Bahamas

Havana

Cuba

Dominican Republic

Antigua and Barbuda

Mexico City

Haiti

Dominica

St. Lucia

Jamaica

Grenada

Belize

Trinidad and Tobago

Guatemala

Honduras

El Salvador

Nicaragua

SOUTH AMERICA

Olmec Chapultec Park

Costa Rica

Panama

Highest mountain: *Mount McKinley,* 20,320 feet (6,194 meters)

Longest river: *Missouri,* 2,540 miles (4,090 kilometers)

Largest desert: *Sonoran,* 70,000 square miles (181,000 square kilometers)

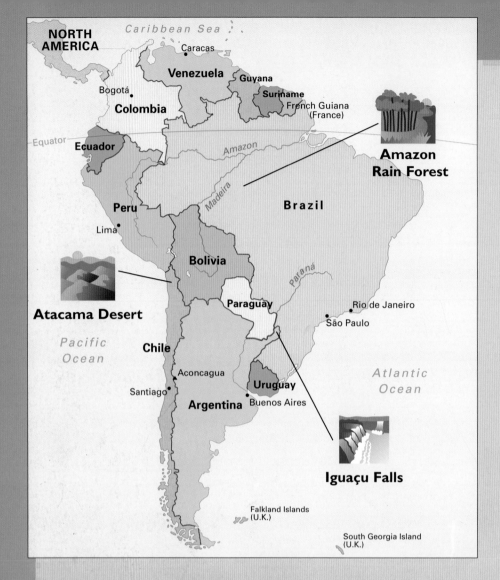

NORTH AMERICA

Caribbean Sea

Caracas

Venezuela

Guyana

Suriname

French Guiana (France)

Bogotá

Colombia

Equator

Ecuador

Amazon

Amazon Rain Forest

Madeira

Peru

Lima

Brazil

Bolivia

Paraná

Atacama Desert

Paraguay

Rio de Janeiro

São Paulo

Pacific Ocean

Chile

Aconcagua

Atlantic Ocean

Santiago

Uruguay

Argentina

Buenos Aires

Iguaçu Falls

Falkland Islands (U.K.)

South Georgia Island (U.K.)

South America

South America is the fourth largest continent. It has tropical rain forests, deserts, snowy peaks, volcanoes, and rolling grasslands. South America has fewer people than North America.

Most of South America lies south of the **equator**. At the north, the continent is joined to North America by a narrow strip of land. The southern part of the continent is close to Antarctica.

South America has 12 countries. The largest country in South America is Brazil. The smallest is Suriname. Most people in South America live in crowded cities.

People travel to South America to see such ancient ruins as Machu Picchu. The Amazon rain forest and Iguaçu Falls are also in South America.

The government of Brazil meets in these congress buildings in the country's capital city, Brasília.

Highest mountain: *Aconcagua* (AH kawng KAH gwah), 22,831 feet (6,959 meters)
Longest river: *Amazon*, 4,000 miles (6,437 kilometers)
Largest desert: *Atacama* (AT uh KAM uh), 51,000 square miles (132,000 square kilometers)

Antarctica

Antarctica is the fifth largest continent. Although Antarctica is larger than Australia, nobody lives there all the time. That is because Antarctica is the coldest and iciest place in the world. The South Pole is located in Antarctica.

The stormy waters of the Atlantic, Indian, and Pacific oceans surround Antarctica. Ships must steer around towering icebergs and break through huge ice fields to reach the continent. On Antarctica, most of the land is buried in ice. This ice can measure thousands of feet thick, about five times as tall as the world's

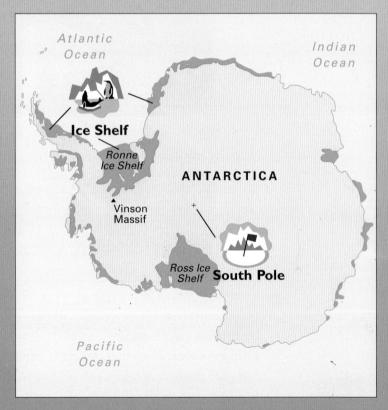

Atlantic Ocean

Indian Ocean

Ice Shelf

Ronne Ice Shelf

ANTARCTICA

Vinson Massif

Ross Ice Shelf **South Pole**

Pacific Ocean

tallest building. But under the ice, Antarctica has mountains, lowlands, and valleys, just like the other continents do. One area near the South Pole is called a "polar desert" because so little snow falls there.

Scientists and travelers visit Antarctica for short periods. Scientists from many nations come to study the continent's animals and plants, ice, and rocks. Only a few small plants and insects can survive on Antarctica's dry land. But many animals, including fish, penguins, whales, and flying birds, live in the cold waters around Antarctica.

The cold **climate** of Antarctica is perfect for these penguins.

Highest mountain:
Vinson Massif (VIHN suhn mah SEEF), 16,864 feet (5,140 meters)
Longest river: *no rivers*
Largest desert: *no true deserts. One area is called a "polar desert."*

Europe

Europe is almost the smallest of the seven continents. Only Australia is smaller. Europe is a region of mountain ranges, rugged coastlines, deep valleys, and plains. Thousands of islands, including Iceland, Corsica, Great Britain, and Ireland, are part of Europe.

All of Europe lies north of the equator. The parts that are farthest north are close

Europe is known for the scenic beauty of its small towns, such as Stryn, Norway.

to the North Pole. Europe is joined to Asia on the east. It is separated from Africa by the Mediterranean Sea. A mountain range called the Alps cuts across the southern part of the continent.

There are 48 countries in Europe. The largest country, Russia, is also the largest country in the world. Part of Russia is in Europe, and part of it is in Asia. Vatican City is the smallest country in the world. It is so small it fits entirely within the city of Rome, Italy.

People from all over the world love to visit Europe for its museums and historic buildings. People also visit Stonehenge, an ancient monument in England.

Highest mountain: *Mount Elbrus*, 18,510 feet (5,642 meters)
Longest river: *Volga*, 2,194 miles (3,531 kilometers)
Largest lake: *Caspian Sea*, 143,250 square miles (371,000 square kilometers)

Indian Ocean

Darwin

Pacific Ocean

Great Sandy Desert

Great Barrier Reef

Australia

Uluru

Great Victoria Desert

Brisbane

Perth

Darling

Adelaide

Sydney

Murray

Canberra

Melbourne

Mount Kosciuszko

Sydney Opera House

Indian Ocean

Tasmania

Australia

Australia is the smallest continent. It is famous for its huge open areas of land, its bright sunshine, and its unusual animals. Australia is a dry land with few people. In fact, it has fewer people than any continent except Antarctica. Australia lies entirely south of the equator. For that reason, it is often called "The Land Down Under."

Australia is completely surrounded by water. It is often grouped with the island of New Zealand and other Pacific islands, which together are called Oceania (OH shee AN ee yuh). Australia is a country, and it is the only country that is also a continent. The island of Tasmania is part of Australia.

In Australia, most people live in cities near the coasts, such as Sydney and Melbourne. But some people live in the outback, a vast area of dry, flatland far from the cities. Here, in the center of the continent, is a very famous rock called Uluru (or Ayers Rock) that is several miles in diameter.

These children live in northern Western Australia.

People go to Australia to hear music at the beautiful Sydney Opera House. Divers visit the Great Barrier Reef, a chain of coral reefs. Other people go to Australia to see kangaroos and koalas.

> **Highest mountain:** *Mount Kosciuszko*
> (KAHZ ee UHS koh), 7,310 feet (2,228 meters)
> **Longest river:** *Murray*, 1,609 miles (2,589 kilometers)
> **Largest desert:** *Great Victoria*, 250,000 square miles (647,000 square kilometers)

TRY THIS! 2

Make Your Own Continent Map

Just as you can learn a lot about a place by looking at a map, you can learn a lot by making your own map. Choose a continent in this chapter that you would like to learn more about, and map it!

You Will Need:

books or encyclopedia
   articles about your
   favorite continent
a pencil
a large sheet of paper
crayons or markers

What To Do:

1. Read about the continent and answer the following questions: What is the tallest mountain? What is the longest river? What is the largest lake or desert? What animals live there? What are the biggest cities?

2. Look through encyclopedias and other books to find different maps of your continent. How do these maps show important information, such as the locations of mountains, rivers, and large cities?

3. Trace or copy the outline of the continent onto the large sheet of paper.

4. Now use a pencil to fill in the map outline. Choose symbols to show cities, rivers, mountains, deserts, and the animals that live in different places on the continent.

5. Color your map. Use green for land, blue for water, and brown for mountains.

6. Decorate the border of your map with pictures of the continent's people, animals, and any other features you want to show.

Now, laminate your map or put it in a plastic cover.

One World

The seven continents are far apart from one another, but they are all part of the earth. No matter how far apart the continents are, the people who live on them are connected because they have the same needs. In addition to needing food, clothing, and a place to live, they all need to learn, to communicate, and to plan for the future.

Years ago, people knew very little about the continents. The only way they could learn about them was by traveling on ships. Today, TV's and computers zip information around the world with the flick of a switch or the click of a mouse. People watching TV in Australia can see

In the 1400's, it took Christopher Columbus two months to sail from Spain to the Bahamas. Today, a jet plane could make the same trip in just a few hours.

Many people in the world like to watch television. These children from Saudi Arabia enjoy a show together.

a person rafting down the Amazon River in South America. A scientist in North America can send an instant message to a scientist in Antarctica by computer.

Yes, the continents are very far apart. But **transportation** and technology have brought the people who live on them much closer together.

Telephones allow people to communicate over long **distances.** Imagine what a person living in Christopher Columbus's time would have thought of that!

Say "Ahalan!" or "Ni hao" to the World

Around the world, people speak more than 6,000 languages. If you learn to say *hello* in just a few of these languages, you could say hello to millions of people! Here are some important words in other languages.

Hello

Arabic	ahalan
Hebrew	shalom
Japanese	konnichiwa
Mandarin Chinese	ni hao
Russian	priven
Swahili	jambo

Goodbye

Arabic	ma'a el salaama
Hebrew	shalom
Japanese	sayonara
Mandarin Chinese	zai jian
Russian	do svidaniya

Please

Arabic	min fadlak
Hebrew	b'vakashah
Japanese	douzo
Russian	pazhaluysta
Swahili	tafadhali

Thank you

Arabic   shokran
Hebrew   todah
Japanese   arigatoo
Mandarin Chinese   xie xie
Russian   spasibo
Swahili   asante

Yes

Arabic   na'am
Hebrew   kein
Japanese   hai
Mandarin Chinese   shi
Russian   da
Swahili   ndiyo

Friend

Arabic   sadik
Hebrew   chaver, chavera
Japanese   tomodachi
Mandarin Chinese   peng you
Swahili   rafiki

School

Arabic   madrassa
Hebrew   beit sefer
Japanese   gakkou
Mandarin Chinese   xue xiao
Russian   shkola
Swahili   shule

31

Mystery Continents

Looking at a globe can help you learn important information about continents. It is also fun! Use a **globe** to play this guessing game with a friend.

You Will Need:

a globe
a long piece of string
  for measuring
  distance
a friend

What To Do:

1. Think of a continent you want to learn more about. Have your friend think of one too. Keep your continents a secret!

2. Take turns finding your continent on the globe. Don't let your friend see which continent you are looking for.

3. Study the continent you chose. Notice important information about it. The questions on the next page might help.

4. Take turns giving clues about the continent to your friend.

5. The first one who guesses the other person's continent wins.

You might want to choose a different continent each time you play this game. Then every time you play you will learn something new!

North America

Europe

Asia

Africa

equator

South America

Australia

Antarctica

Questions to help you make up clues about your continent.

• Does the continent have a large mountain chain, river, or desert that you notice right away?

• Which ocean is the continent near?

• Which continent is farthest away from it? Use the string to find out.

• Is the continent close to—or far away from—the North Pole? The South Pole?

• Is the continent completely surrounded by water?

• Does the continent touch another continent?

• What other continents are close to it?

• Does the continent have lots of countries?

• Is the continent above or below the equator? Or does the equator cross through the continent? If it does, is most of the continent above or below the equator?

How Will You Get There?

To get around your neighborhood, you probably take a walk or ride your bike. But in parts of the world where houses stand on stilts and are surrounded by water, children paddle canoes from house to house.

To travel longer distances, people use other kinds of transportation. Buses and trains take many people from city to city, or even across one or more countries.

People can travel on rivers, canals, lakes, and oceans in boats of all shapes and sizes. There are many different kinds of airplanes, too. Some are big, some are small, and some are even fast enough to jet from one side of the world to the other in just hours!

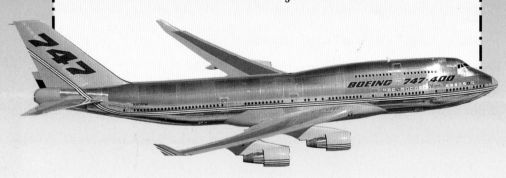

What Is Wheel Power?

If walking is too slow, use wheels! A bicycle, skateboard, or pair of in-line skates can take you places you want to go. You can roll as far as the roads or paths—and your legs—will take you!

In China, there are not many cars. Most roads are unpaved, and few Chinese people can afford to buy a car. So most people get around on bicycles. There are so many cyclists that special traffic police are needed to direct them on their way.

Some people use their wheels—and their legs—to take other people where they want to go. Pedicabs are popular in India and other parts of Asia. Comfortable seats at the back can hold two people, while the cyclist pulls them along.

Using muscle power does not cost a lot of money, and it can be fun, too. Be sure you know the rules of the road, and always pay attention to traffic. Keep your bike and safety equipment in good working order so you are ready to roll anytime.

an owner of a cycle-rickshaw in India

Why Are There Roads?

This mountain pass in the South Tyrol, Austria, is a challenge to drivers.

The road zigzags farther and farther upward. You peer out of the car window and gulp as you look back. It's a very long way down!

You are traveling over a mountain pass in the South Tyrol (tuh ROHL), Austria. It is too steep to go straight up, so the roads to the top wind backward and forward like a slithering snake.

Today, there are roads across all the countries of the world. Some are little more than dirt trails, and others are six-lane or eight-lane highways that carry heavy traffic in each direction.

In Western Australia, roads are strong enough to support these powerful trucks.

This icy road winds through Keystone Canyon in Alaska.

Roads of some sort have existed for thousands of years. Often a road started as a rough trail—the easiest route from one place to another. Over the years, the feet of people and animals wore it down until it became a smooth, wide path. As towns grew, the paths became wider still. Some were covered with gravel, pebbles, or other materials to make them permanent roads.

In Uganda, a country in Africa, people take their banana crop to market along a dirt road.

Why Ride Cars and Motorcycles?

This African man lives in a traditional Nigerian village but uses a modern motorbike for transportation.

Before automobiles were invented, people walked, cycled, rode animals, or rode vehicles pulled by animals to work or to visit friends and family. So people usually lived near their work and family.

The invention of the car allowed people to live farther away from their work. Today, cars zoom over roads and highways to take

people to work. Cars also take people to the homes of friends and family. Many people drive to vacation spots such as theme parks, national parks, mountains, or seashores.

There are more than 450 million passenger cars in the world. While cars help people in many ways, they cause problems, too. These problems include accidents, pollution, and frustrating traffic jams. Many people try to help solve these problems by carpooling, or sharing rides with several people. Some cities set aside special highway lanes to be used only by carpooling passengers.

In some countries, motorcycles are a popular way to get to work. Most motorcycles are less expensive than cars and take up less space. Many police officers use motorcycles because they are small enough to move easily through traffic.

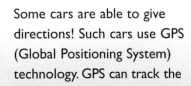

KNOW It All!

Some cars are able to give directions! Such cars use GPS (Global Positioning System) technology. GPS can track the location of a car using a satellite. A device installed in the car allows it to map out a route based upon the car's location.

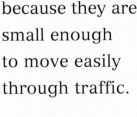

How Do People Travel Across Snow and Ice?

Dogsleds are used to cross huge icy areas in Alaska.

In Canada, winters are long and cold. In some parts of the country, deep snow covers the ground for months at a time, and it is hard to go from place to place. Some of Canada's people have solved this problem by using sleds pulled by dogs.

The sleds are handy, but today, some people use snowmobiles to move heavy loads. A snowmobile is a kind of sled on skis, with a motor to push it through even the thickest snow. The driver uses handlebars to steer the snowmobile.

Another way of moving through frozen places is to put on skates. People travel on skates across ice in cold northern countries, such as Finland, Norway, Sweden, and Russia.

The Lapps of northern Europe use both old and new ways to cross the snow-covered ground. Some use skis to travel with their herds of reindeer, while their belongings are strapped onto a sled pulled by reindeer. Others use snowmobiles, and some even use helicopters.

The Lapps use reindeer to pull their sleds.

An Inuit woman in Canada uses a snowmobile to carry home the supplies brought by the airplane.

This man rides a reed boat on Lake Titicaca, in South America.

How Do People Travel Across Water?

Some of the first boats were made thousands of years ago by the ancient Egyptians. They built their boats out of a reed called **papyrus** (puh PY ruhs).

Today, the same kind of boat making still goes on. Some people cut tall reeds. They bend and weave them into fishing boats.

These people are riding a small Egyptian sailboat ferry across the water.

Other people build long, thin boats called canoes. They build or carve the boats from wood. Both kinds of boats are light enough to carry across the mud to the river's edge.

Today, many boats are complicated machines. They are built to go on long journeys in any kind of weather, and they often carry heavy loads.

Ferries are like taxis. They carry people and sometimes cars across a body of water.

Ocean liners are much bigger. They carry people across an ocean, sometimes traveling for many days.

The Queen Mary 2 pulling into port in Fort Lauderdale, Florida.

All Aboard!

You're at a place where there are lots of things to see, hear, smell, and taste. You can hear the cawing of hungry sea birds.

Harbors often create lovely scenes, such as this one in the Cyclades Islands of Greece.

You can see boats loading and unloading, tiny tugboats hauling enormous ships, and sailors getting ready for a cruise. Where are you? At a **harbor!**

Boats and ships begin and end their voyages at a harbor. A harbor is a protected body of water. Some harbors are partly surrounded by land. The land protects them from dangerous ocean waves and strong winds. Other harbors are built near narrow channels of water. On open coasts, huge walls are built to protect a harbor.

At a harbor, you might smell the salty air and motor fuel. At small harbors, people dock and refuel their boats. These harbors may have ramps that people use to unload the boats from their trailers. Other harbors are big enough to hold many large ships and barges.

Clang clang clang. The captains of boats and ships carefully move their vessels around the clanging colored buoys (BOO eez). The buoys warn them of dangerous places, such as shallow water and rocks.

If you are lucky, the harbor might even have a snack bar with delicious seafood to taste!

How Do People Travel on Sand?

All is quiet except for the tinkling of harness bells and the shifting of sand, as the great animals lift their feet. Everywhere you look there is sand—as far as the eye can see. There is no road to follow, not even a track, but a string of camels winds its way across the vast desert.

A Tuareg tribesman and his wife lead their caravan of camels across the Sahara in Africa.

A string of camels carrying goods is called a **caravan** (KAIR uh van). Camel caravans are still a common sight in the desert. But, small airplanes and sturdy all-terrain vehicles are now used in some desert places.

A camel caravan may make its way to Timbuktu in Mali, western Africa. Timbuktu is near the southern edge of the Sahara. Every year from December to May, great camel caravans gather there. People come from many places to trade goods.

The camel is the ideal animal to use for transportation in a desert, because its wide feet do not sink into the sand. Also,

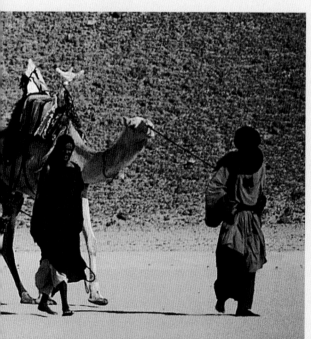

camels can go for several days without water and use fat in their humps to keep them alive. If you think the desert seems like an ocean of sand, you can see why camels are often called "ships of the desert."

Why Do People Ride Buses?

The bus driver eyes the back of the school bus. "Stay in your seats," he says firmly and loudly enough to be heard over the roar of the engine and the noisy chatter of the children. Many people recognize school buses by their flashing lights. But buses come in all different sizes and colors, depending on how they

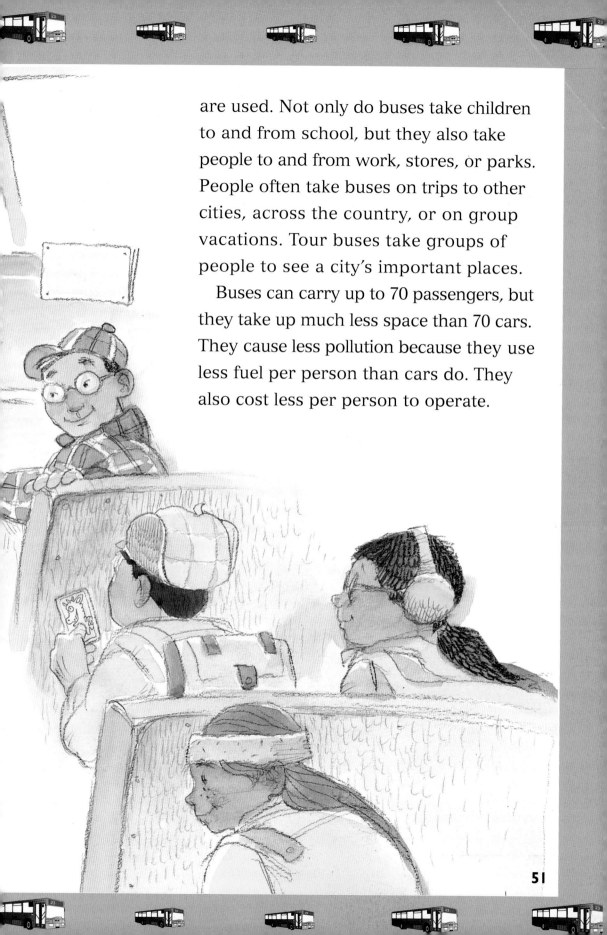

are used. Not only do buses take children to and from school, but they also take people to and from work, stores, or parks. People often take buses on trips to other cities, across the country, or on group vacations. Tour buses take groups of people to see a city's important places.

Buses can carry up to 70 passengers, but they take up much less space than 70 cars. They cause less pollution because they use less fuel per person than cars do. They also cost less per person to operate.

Why Do People Ride Trains?

They can move people at speeds of more than 170 miles (275 kilometers) per hour. They carry goods weighing thousands of tons across a **continent**. Almost every country has them, and many children

In France, many people travel from the suburbs to jobs and cultural activities in the city.

collect toy models of them. What are they? Trains!

Every day, in many places throughout the world, trains carry thousands of people along railroad tracks. People who want to travel from one city to another use trains. Many people who live in one town and work in another take a train to work. Some trains make longer trips. They have beds for sleeping and serve meals in dining cars.

Subways are underground city trains that zoom people from place to place. Elevated trains, or els, crisscross a city on tracks that are built above the streets.

Every day, thousands of commuters board trains in the New York City subway system.

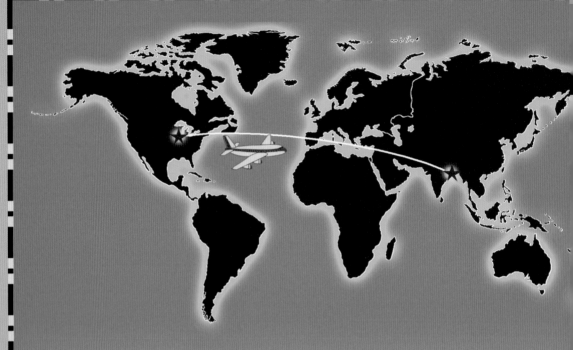

Why Do People Fly?

Airplanes and helicopters are two ways to get far in a hurry. They carry people and goods thousands of feet above the ground.

The first thing you might notice about an airplane is its wings. When an airplane starts moving, the special shape of its wings helps it rise in the air and fly. Under the airplane wings are its engines. The fastest planes have jet engines that help them travel halfway around the world—

from Chicago, Illinois, to Kolkata (Calcutta), India—in about 15 hours! Sometimes people can watch a movie, listen to music, or eat a meal or a snack while flying in the clouds.

Helicopters do not have the same type of wings that airplanes do. A helicopter is powered by whirling blades that lift it into the sky. Helicopters are not as fast as some airplanes, but they can change directions and land more easily. They can fly forward, upward, and sideways. They can also hover, or stay in one place in the air.

One of the world's largest passenger airplanes is the Airbus A380. The A380 can carry more than 550 passengers.

What Is an Airport?

The day has finally arrived! You are at the airport and about to board the plane that will take you on your dream vacation. There are many things you need to do at the airport before takeoff.

At the check-in counter, an airline worker checks you in, tells you which seat is yours, and gives you a boarding pass. Your luggage is put onto a moving belt. It carries your suitcase through rubber flaps in the wall to large bins that are wheeled to the plane. The agent tells you which departure gate your plane will leave from.

At the airport, you and other travelers may also pass through a gate that has special machines. The machines make sure nobody is carrying anything dangerous.

At the departure gate, another airline worker takes your boarding pass. You are ready to board the plane.

You may have to walk through a tunnel or upstairs to get to the plane. When you enter the plane, a flight attendant helps you find your seat. You find a bin above your head in which to put your coats, small bags, or toys. Of course, you fasten your seatbelt!

Suddenly the plane's engines roar to life. The plane is moving! It moves slowly, at first, then faster and faster down a long paved path called a runway. Finally, you're up! Sit back and enjoy the ride.

TRY THIS! 1

It's a good idea to get to the airport an hour or more before the plane is supposed to take off. Bring a quiet toy or a book to help pass the time. You might also want to bring a journal to write down everything you see on your trip. Put stickers or tape on your luggage, especially if you check it instead of carrying it on the plane yourself. That will help you spot it after your flight.

Walk, Ride, or Fly?

Could you cycle to an island? Would you take a plane to school? The type of transportation you use depends on where you are going, how far away it is, and how fast you want to get there. Sometimes it even depends on the weather! The map on these pages shows a small town called Our Town. It has lots of places to visit. Take a look at all the different places on the map. Now turn the page and test your travel I.Q.!

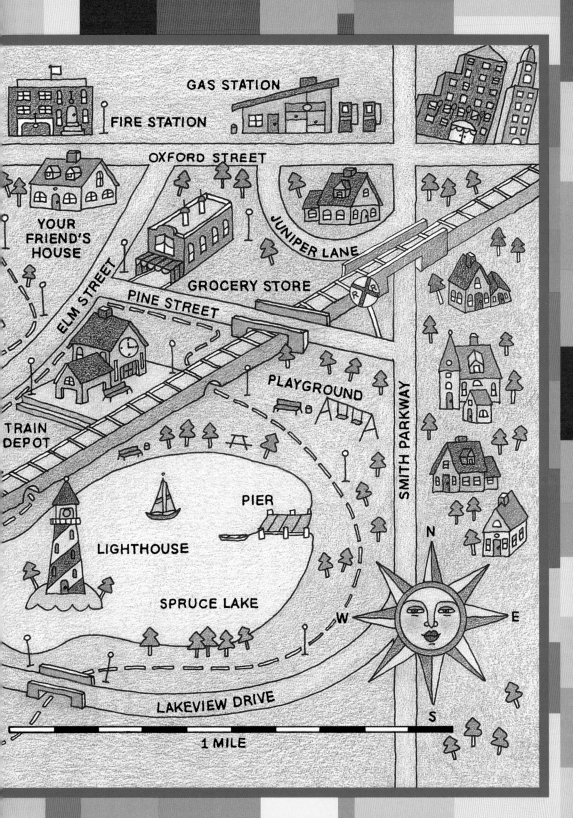

GAS STATION

FIRE STATION

OXFORD STREET

YOUR FRIEND'S HOUSE

JUNIPER LANE

ELM STREET

PINE STREET

GROCERY STORE

PLAYGROUND

SMITH PARKWAY

TRAIN DEPOT

PIER

LIGHTHOUSE

SPRUCE LAKE

N

W   E

S

LAKEVIEW DRIVE

1 MILE

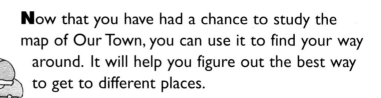

Now that you have had a chance to study the map of Our Town, you can use it to find your way around. It will help you figure out the best way to get to different places.

1. You want to pick up your friend at the playground and then go to the playing field. But you're not allowed to cross busy streets. How can you get where you want to go?

2. What shortcut could you take if you were walking from the school to the grocery store?

3. How would get to the lighthouse from the pier? Which roads would you take to get closest to the pier if you were coming from the airport and you needed to buy gas?

4. How far away is Roger's Bay from this town? What is a good way to get there if you don't have a car?

5. If you wanted to get from the school to the toy store, how might you go there on a warm, sunny day? In the pouring rain, could you take a train?

6. Name the places you could visit if you rode your bike along the whole bike path. Could you go to the post office without leaving the bike path?

Answers:

1. Ride your bike along the bike path. It passes the playing field and the playground, and it goes under the busy streets.

2. across the playing field

3. You'd take a boat. From the airport, you'd take a car south on Main Street. Turn east on Oxford Street, and then turn south onto Smith Parkway to get closest to the pier.

4. 50 miles. Go by train.

5. On a nice day, you could ride your bike, walk, or skate. In the rain, you'd want to get a ride in a car because the train doesn't stop at the toy store or the school.

6. Library, lake, pier, playground, train depot, grocery store, playing field, your friend's house, and your house. No, you could not get to the post office on the bike path.

61

Where in the World?

Airplanes, trains, and ships can take you almost anywhere in the world. You can fly in a plane to a crowded city in Japan, sail on a boat down the Amazon River in South America, or ride on a train across country.

But did you know that you can feel as if you've been to these exciting places without even leaving your own house? Reading books and looking at pictures can make you feel as if you've been there!

The World in a Day

Kyle was bored and grumpy. All of his friends were away on vacation, and he had nothing to do. "Some school vacation," Kyle grumbled as he slumped into his chair and started eating his breakfast. He was about to start munching on his Crispy Crunchies when he spotted a stack of cards tied with a red ribbon.

When he untied the ribbon, Kyle saw that the cards were postcards. They were from far-off places: Japan, Kenya, and Brazil. Kyle was puzzled.

"Grandmother, what is this?" Kyle asked.

His grandmother came and stood beside him. "Hmm," she said. "It looks like you won't be bored today! Better go put on your gym shoes. You're in for an adventure. First stop, Kenya!"

Kyle followed his grandmother toward the living room. In the hallway, she stopped him and handed him the postcard from Kenya. It showed an elephant walking across a grassy plain in the sun. Kyle looked up and could not believe his eyes. Grandmother had turned the living room into an African **plain**. On the walls were pictures of lions, elephants, and zebras. On the table sat an African mask and a bowl carved out of wood.

Kyle was amazed. He never knew his grandmother had such wonderful things. "Jambo (JAHM boh)," his grandmother said. "That's Swahili for 'hello.'

"In Kenya, cassava (kuh SAH vuh) is an important food. It's a root vegetable like a potato. Here, try some." Kyle took a big bite. It tasted like sweet potatoes.

Then his grandmother handed Kyle a book called *African Safari*. It had pictures of people and wild animals. His grandmother touched his shoulder. "You can read that book when you return from your journey," she said.

"OK, time for our next adventure," she continued. "On to Tokyo!" Kyle clutched the book under his arm and followed his grandmother to his grandparents' room.

"Konnichiwa (koh nee chee wah)," she said, bowing. Then she handed him the postcard from Tokyo. The postcard showed two women hiding their faces behind beautiful paper fans.

Kyle looked into his grandparents' room. Paper fans covered the walls. The pillows from the chair were on the floor. On the bed was the most amazing kite

Kyle had ever seen. Kyle wanted to touch it. "Wait!" his grandmother said. "You must take your shoes off before you go inside. That is the custom in Japan." Kyle did as he was told.

Then his grandmother placed a tray with a teapot and tiny cups on the table. Kyle drank the tea. It didn't taste anything like the tea he was used to. It had no cream and no sugar!

After they finished their tea, his grandmother handed Kyle another book. This book was called *A Journey Through Japan*. The cover showed a kite festival

with dozens of kites like the one on his
grandparents' bed.

As Kyle followed his grandmother out
to the yard, he heard lively music. "Here,
put this on," she said and handed Kyle a
mask covered with bright feathers.

"We went to Rio de Janeiro for
Carnival," she said. "It was one
big party—four days of dancing,
singing, and parades. In
Brazil, a favorite food is
black beans with rice.
Here, try this. It's a
little spicy." Kyle
tried the beans.
Were they hot!

Then his
grandmother
handed Kyle
another book.
This one was called
Discovering Brazil.

"Well, sir, that's the end of our very quick trip. But you can do some more traveling on your own."

Kyle didn't care if it rained tomorrow—or the next day, either. If it did, he would just pick up one of his grandmother's books and take another trip!

Be an armchair traveler. Pick a faraway country. Look for books that will help you answer these questions:

• What language do the people speak?

• Do the children go to a school like yours? Say why it might be different.

• What are some of the names people give to children?

• What kinds of work can children do when they grow up?

• Can both women and men do these jobs?

The Clothes People Wear

No one knows exactly why—or when—people first wore clothes. But early people probably began to wear clothes for the same reasons that we wear clothes today. Clothes keep us warm and dry. Some people—nurses, police officers, priests, and many others— wear clothes that show who they are or what they do. And sometimes we wear clothes that make us look like part of a group or clothes that make us stand out in a crowd.

young Buddhist monks wearing orange robes

Think about your own clothes as you read the following pages about clothes worn by people around the world. How are they like the clothes you wear, and how are they different? What do you like about the different kinds of clothing? When you are finished looking at all of the clothing, choose a kind you would like to try. Then, draw a picture of yourself wearing it.

a Ndebele woman in South Africa

children in bright colors, ready to play

Clothes for Cold Climates

Brrrrrrrr, it's cold outside! You want to go out and play. What do you wear to keep warm? Perhaps you wear a heavy coat, hat, scarf, gloves or mittens, and warm boots.

Some people must wear warm clothes most of the time. People in northern Canada, Greenland, and other places that are far north live in **climates** that are cold most of the year. In these cold regions, people wear heavy clothes made of fur or wool.

An **Inuit** man wears clothes made from animal skins. A hooded jacket, or parka, protects the top part of an Inuit's body. Can you guess what he wears under his jacket? Another jacket! He also wears two pairs of pants to protect his legs. The heat from his body stays between the two layers of clothes, and this helps to keep him warm. Thick fur mittens protect his hands, and he wears sealskin boots on his feet.

An Inuit man of northern North America wears a furry parka and trousers.

Clothes for Hot Climates

In India's hot climate, most people wear light, loose clothes.

You are midway through your soccer game, and the sun is beating down on you. Sweat drips off your forehead. To keep cool, you are wearing a T-shirt and shorts.

In warm places, people wear clothes made of a lightweight material, such as cotton or linen, to stay cool. Much of the clothing in warm regions is white or light-colored, because these colors reflect the sun's rays. Darker colors absorb heat from the sun, so they make a person feel hotter.

A man rides a long-legged camel across the Sahara. The sun burns bright and hot. This man is a Tuareg (TWAH rehg). He raises animals in the desert. A light blue robe covers him from shoulders to ankles. The loose folds of the robe shield him from the hot sun. They also let air flow around his body, helping to keep him cool. He has a long cloth wrapped around his head. Part of the cloth can be pulled over his mouth and nose to keep out blowing sand. Just as your lightweight clothes keep you cool in the hot sun, this man's clothing protects him from the weather.

This Tuareg man can pull the extra cloth of his headdress over his mouth and nose to keep out blowing sand.

TRY THIS!
2

Weave Your Own Friendship Bracelet

In many countries, people make rugs, baskets, and blankets. They make them by **weaving.** Weavers use a machine called a **loom** to cross threads over and under one another. The threads are made of cotton, silk, or even grass. Sometimes the threads are colored with dyes made from plants. You can make a simple hand loom out of straws and use it to weave a bracelet for your friend.

You Will Need:

2½ feet (1 meter) thin cotton twine
2 plastic drinking straws, each cut in half
different-colored yarn

What To Do:

1. Cut the twine into four equal pieces and thread each piece through a straw. Tie the four ends above the straws into a knot.

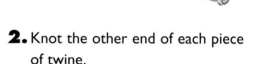

2. Knot the other end of each piece of twine.

3. Tie a piece of yarn to the twine just below the top knot.

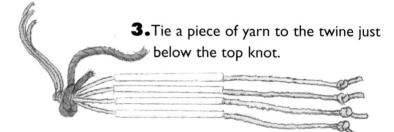

4. Weave the yarn under and over the straws from side to side. Use your fingers to push up each row of yarn onto the twine and slide the straws down. To change colors, tie a new piece of yarn to the end of the first one and weave in the loose ends.

5. Make your bracelet long enough to tie around your friend's wrist. When your bracelet is the length you want, remove the straws. To fasten the last row, tie the end of the yarn to the piece of the twine. Then tie a knot with the two pieces of twine on the left. Repeat with the pair on the right. Finally, tie together the four twine pieces with another knot.

Now you are ready to give your bracelet to a friend!

The Work People Do

People have always had to work. Early people hunted animals and gathered plants. Some people fished. Later, they learned to farm. They made their own clothes, tools, and furniture. They swapped some of the things they made, grew, or caught for other things they needed. This is called **bartering.** Then people began to use money. Some people paid others to work for them. Workers used that money to buy what they needed.

A Moroccan family works in the field.

78

A teacher leads her students on a field trip.

In some places in the world today, people still live as the early people did. They hunt, fish, or farm in small groups near their homes, and they make everything they need for everyday life.

In other places, people who farm or fish sell much of what they grow or catch. Some people make things for other people to buy. They are craftworkers and factory workers. Some people work as teachers, scientists, nurses, and doctors. They help other people.

Year after year, people learn, discover, and invent things. As they do this, they find different kinds of work to do.

Homes for All Places

Zulu people of South Africa build homes of reeds and straw.

Steep roofs let snow easily slide off these colorful houses in Norway.

Some of the very first houses were caves. They had walls and ceilings that kept out wind, rain, and prowling animals. They had floors where people could sit or sleep.

In time, people learned to build different kinds of homes. They needed homes that were right for the place where they lived. They used materials they found nearby.

In dry places, houses were made of mud or clay. Where there was plenty of wood, people built houses of logs or boards. On grassy plains, they built homes of dry grass.

People who lived near rivers made rafts or houseboats, or built their houses on stilts.

Today, people still build homes that are right for the place where they live. People who live in very hot places need houses that keep them cool. People in the frozen north need houses that keep the cold out.

On the banks of the Amazon River in Peru, houses are built on stilts to protect them from flooding.

In such large cities as Chicago, many people live in high-rise apartments.

In Hong Kong, many people live in boats on the harbor.

Our homes—even apartment buildings—have much in common with those first caves. They protect us against the weather and give us a safe place to sit and sleep.

What House Will You Build?

Here is your chance to design your own house. For each place listed below, decide which materials from the next page you would use to build your house. *See answers on page 83.*

Where You Live

1. An area close to a swamp. Floods occur quite often.

2. A very rainy place.

3. A dry rural place with few trees.

4. A crowded big city with buildings that are homes for many people.

5. A place close to a river, lake, sea, or ocean.

stilt house

mud house

Materials for a House

A. mud for making bricks

B. wooden poles on which to build your house

C. waterproof shingles for your roof

D. concrete bricks and steel beams

E. wood, fiberglass, or aluminum for making a house that floats

cottage

apartment building

houseboats

Famous Places

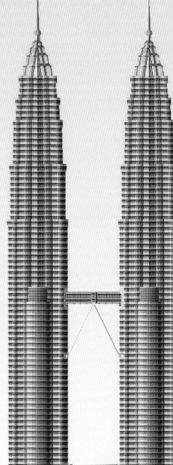

When you travel to places near and far, you can see with your own eyes the work of great architects and engineers. They are the people who have designed and built skyscrapers, churches and **temples,** castles, and bridges.

When you travel, you can see the wonders of nature, too. You can gaze at magnificent canyons, mountains that seem to reach the clouds, and rivers so wide you can't see the other side.

What Are Castles?

Some of the world's most amazing buildings were built for protection, not

The famous French author Michel de Montaigne lived his whole life in this castle.

beauty. Hundreds of years ago, people in different parts of the world had many rulers. The rulers often fought each other. Powerful rulers built castles to live in with their family, helpers, priests, soldiers—and farm animals!

Many of the castles were made of stone. Often they were built around an open courtyard. They had high walls that could be 30 feet (10 meters) thick to protect against enemies. Some castles had towers at each corner.

Sometimes the walls were surrounded with deep, wide ditches that were usually filled with water. These were called moats. To protect the castle, guards looked out from the towers and walked along the tops of the walls. They hid behind stone fences called battlements and shot arrows at attackers. When visitors came, the guards would lower a drawbridge so people could walk or ride across the moat. Then the visitors would have to pass a gatehouse.

Inside, there was a large great room where people met and ate meals. A huge fire in the fireplace took away the chill. So did tapestries, or hanging cloths, placed around the castle walls. People spread sweet-smelling plants on the floors and changed them every month.

The king slept in this bedroom in the Linderhof Palace in Bavaria, Germany.

The Tower of London has been a fort, a palace, and a prison. Today it is a museum.

Castles had a kitchen, a chapel in which to pray, and apartments for the family. They also had a barracks, or sleeping room, for soldiers. Many had dungeons in which to keep prisoners.

In many places around the world, ancient castles still stand. One is the Tower of London on the River Thames in London, England. This group of stone buildings has a wall and moat surrounding it. The Tower of London was first built as a castle in the 1000's. In later times, it was a palace and a prison. Today it is a museum.

The Loire (lwahr) Valley in France is famous for its castles, called chateaux (shah TOHZ) in French. One of the oldest French chateaux is in Angers (ahn ZHAY). Visitors can still see the remains of the 17 towers and the moat. This chateau was built in the early 1200's.

In Syria, near the northern border of present-day Lebanon, is a castle called Krak des Chevaliers (KRAHK day shuh VAH lyay). This fortress was built during the 1100's.

The Chateau D'Angers is one of many famous castles in France's Loire Valley.

In Syria stands the Krak des Chevaliers, a castle built during the 1100's.

The picture on these pages shows a typical castle. Find the following parts of the castle.

a. A moat surrounded the castle. It was filled with water to keep enemies out.

b. Strong towers helped soldiers defend the castle. People also lived in them.

c. Soldiers hid from enemies behind battlements.

d. The outdoor space inside the castle was the courtyard.

e. Meals were cooked in the kitchen.

f. The chapel was where people prayed.

g. The gatehouse was where soldiers raised and lowered the gate.

h. The dungeon was where prisoners were kept.

i. The great hall was the room that most people used during the day.

j. A drawbridge crossed the moat. It could be pulled up when an enemy was near.

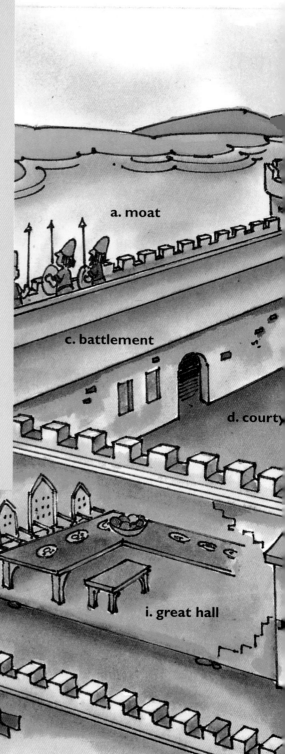

a. moat

c. battlement

d. courty

h. dungeon

i. great hall

b. tower

e. kitchen

f. chapel

g. gatehouse

j. drawbridge

Home Is Their Castle

A stone bridge over a moat leads to the imperial castle in Tokyo, Japan.

Many castles were designed as homes for rulers rather than as fortresses. Many of the world's most famous and fancy palaces were built hundreds of years ago.

The rulers of the United Kingdom live at Windsor Castle when they are not in nearby London. William the Conqueror built a castle in that place about 1070. Since then, many rulers have added to the castle, which now covers 9 acres (3.6 hectares). It has 15 majestic towers and a beautiful chapel.

Another famous castle lies on a hill in the city of Osaka, Japan. The elegant Osaka Castle was built during the 1500's. Visitors can still see three of the original towers as well as the castle's main gate.

A famous palace is in Versailles (ver SY), France. The Palace of Versailles is more than 1/4 mile (0.4 kilometer) long and has

The magnificent Hall of Mirrors thrills visitors to the palace of Versailles in France.

about 1,300 rooms. It was built by the French King Louis XIV in the 1600's.

To see a real fairy-tale castle, go to Neuschwanstein (noy SHVAHN shtyn) Castle in Germany. It has a walled courtyard, spires on its roof, and a blue arched ceiling decorated with stars. Built for King Ludwig II in the 1860's, the castle is now a popular place to visit.

KNOW It All! This castle, Neuschwanstein, was the inspiration for the make-believe Fantasyland castles at Disney theme parks.

The government of Andorra, one of the world's smallest countries, meets in the House of the Valleys.

Where Do Leaders Work?

Many people work in tall skyscrapers, small office buildings, or tiny stores. And people who run governments often work in places that are works of art that look powerful or grand. The buildings in which they work might be gleaming white mansions, majestic palaces, or buildings tucked behind the walls of a fortress. Here are some famous government buildings around the world.

The White House, in Washington, D.C., is the home and the office of the United States president.

Both houses of the Indian
parliament meet in the
Parliament House in New Delhi.

The Kremlin, in Moscow, is an
old fort. It contains many of
Russia's government buildings.

The British government meets
in the Houses of Parliament in
London, England.

The Eiffel Tower, in Paris, France, was built for the 1889 World's Fair.

What Are Modern Wonders of the World?

People have built many incredible structures. Some soar to dizzying heights. Others cross huge lakes or rivers. Here are just a few modern wonders you can see around the world.

The Eiffel Tower is a huge iron tower in Paris. Built for a world's fair in 1889, the tower rises 984 feet (300 meters). You can take stairs or elevators to the top. The Eiffel Tower was the highest structure in the world for many years.

In Toronto, Canada, stands the CN Tower, one of the world's highest free-standing structures. The communications and observation tower stands 1,815 feet (553 meters) high. It was completed in 1976.

At night, the CN Tower and SkyDome brighten the Toronto sky.

The Akashi Kaikyo Bridge in
Japan took 10 years to build.

In 1998, the Akashi Kaikyo Bridge
opened in Japan. Its main suspension span,
the world's longest, stretches 6,527 feet
(1,990 meters) across the Akashi Strait.
The bridge took about 10 years to build.

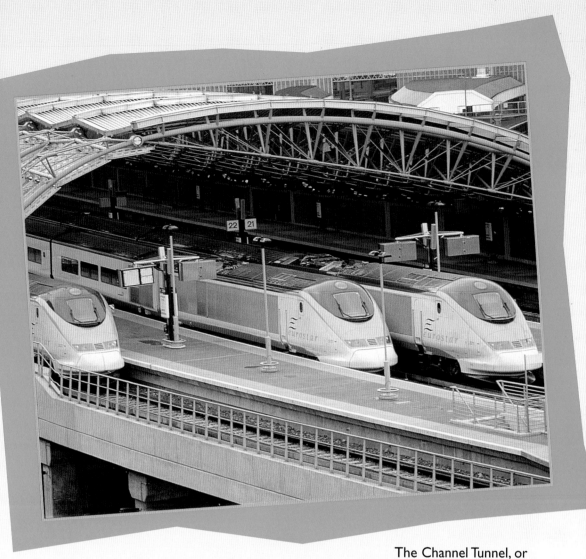

The Channel Tunnel, or "Chunnel," carries traffic between the United Kingdom and France.

The Channel Tunnel is an undersea railway that connects the United Kingdom with France. It opened in 1994. Fast electric trains carry cars and buses, people and goods through the tunnel, under the English Channel. The journey can take less than 35 minutes.

The Suez Canal waterway joins the Mediterranean Sea and the Red Sea in Egypt. It is 118 miles (190 kilometers) long and 64 feet (19.5 meters) deep. When the canal opened in 1869, ships traveling between England and India no longer had to sail around Africa. This shortened the trip by 5,000 miles (8,000 kilometers)!

Another famous canal was built between North America and South America to link the Atlantic and Pacific oceans. When the Panama Canal was finished in 1914, it

The Suez Canal, in Egypt, is a shortcut for ships traveling between Europe and Asia.

A ship enters the locks of the Panama Canal, in Central America.

shortened the trip between New York City, New York, and San Francisco, California, by 9,000 miles (14,500 kilometers). Ships no longer had to sail around South America.

Wonders of Long Ago

Did you know that there are monuments, tombs, and huge walls that were built hundreds or even thousands of years ago? Sometimes only small parts, or ruins, of these places remain. But you can still visit them today.

Ancient peoples built Stonehenge, in England, more than 3,500 years ago.

In England, tourists and scientists alike are amazed by Stonehenge, a group of huge, rough-cut stones set in circles. Scientists believe that ancient people built Stonehenge as a gathering place. Much of the monument is gone, but scientists think that when it was first built, an earth wall about 320 feet (98 meters) across circled it. Thirty blocks of gray sandstone stood like guards 13 1/2 feet (4 meters) above the ground.

Another wonder from long ago is the Great Pyramid at Giza in Egypt. Pyramids were built by Egyptians about 4,500 years ago as tombs for their kings. The Great Pyramid contains more than 2 million stone blocks.

The pyramids of Egypt at Giza were one of the Seven Wonders of the Ancient World.

The Inca people built Machu Picchu in what is now Peru during the late 1400's.

In Peru, you can visit the ruins of Machu Picchu (MAH choo PEEK choo), which was once a walled city. It was built during the late 1400's by the Inca and was probably a home for the Inca royal family.

The longest structure ever built, the Great Wall of China, stretches nearly 4,000 miles (6,400 kilometers). The wall was built to protect the northern Chinese border against enemies. Most of the wall that stands today was built in the 1400's.

The Great Wall of China stretches for thousands of miles.

This tall stone tower is part of the remains of an ancient African city called Great Zimbabwe.

Another famous ruin is the Colosseum in Rome. The structure was completed in A.D. 80. From that time until 404, the Colosseum was a place where people could watch fights between gladiators who were slaves or paid fighters. Battles between men and wild animals and other events entertained Romans. The Colosseum was later abandoned. Many of its stones were used to build other structures.

The Colosseum was the largest outdoor theater in ancient Rome. It could seat

Ancient Greeks built the Parthenon to honor the goddess Athena. It stands on top of a hill called the Acropolis.

The Colosseum, in Rome, is one of the finest examples of Roman architecture.

about 50,000 people. It is made of brick and concrete and is surrounded by 80 entrances.

The Parthenon is a famous ruin perched on a hill in Athens, Greece. It was constructed between 447 and 432 B.C. The Parthenon was a temple built to honor the Greek goddess Athena.

The Parthenon is shaped like a rectangle. It stands about 60 feet (18 meters) high. When the Parthenon was built, it had many brightly colored statues and sculptured panels that showed stories from ancient Greece. Today, many of those statues are at museums in Athens and in London, England.

What Are National Monuments?

Around the world, thousands of buildings, statues, and parks help us remember the past and honor people who made a difference in the world. These places are called **national monuments.**

One of the world's most famous monuments is the Statue of Liberty in New York Harbor. This majestic copper sculpture of a woman holding a torch towers 151 feet (46 meters). A stairway inside the statue lets visitors look out through Liberty's crown. For immigrants who enter the United States through New York Harbor, the statue is a **symbol** of freedom and opportunity. The statue was a

The Statue of Liberty is in New York Harbor.

The Dinosaur National Monument is in Colorado and Utah.

gift from France to the United States in 1885.

At Dinosaur National Monument in the United States, tourists can see fossils of prehistoric reptiles. This national monument in Colorado and Utah also has canyons cut by the Green and Yampa rivers.

One of the greatest battles ever won by the British navy is remembered with a huge statue of Admiral Horatio Nelson at Trafalgar Square in London. Nelson was killed in the battle, but his statue has become one of the world's famous landmarks.

The Nelson monument stands at Trafalgar Square in London, England.

In the center of Hiroshima, Japan, a huge sculpture stands near the ruins of a building destroyed during a nuclear bomb attack. The ruined building, known as the Atomic Bomb Dome, and the sculpture are part of Peace Memorial Park. The monument serves as a reminder of the atomic bomb that was dropped on the city during World War II.

Peace Memorial Park is in Hiroshima, Japan.

What Are Famous Skyscrapers?

Superman may be able to leap over tall buildings in a single bound, but most people are amazed when they see them from the ground. Skyscrapers first appeared during the late 1800's in Chicago and New York. Builders could fit more offices in one area by building upward. The 10-story Home Insurance Building in Chicago, built from 1884 to 1885, became the first skyscraper with a metal frame.

In the 1940's and 1950's, German architect Ludwig Mies van der Rohe became famous for his glass and steel skyscrapers. His most famous structure is the Seagram Building in New York City. This skyscraper has bronze walls and bronze-colored windows.

TRY THIS! 1

Name the 'Scrapers

Read about some of the world's tallest skyscrapers below. Can you tell by the descriptions which is which?

1. It has 110 stories and is 1,450 feet (442 meters) high. This rectangular giant of a building towers above Chicago, Illinois. It is the tallest building in the United States.

2. When this twin-towered structure was completed in 1996, it beat out Chicago's giant building as the world's tallest building. It rises 1,483 feet (452 meters) in Kuala Lumpur, Malaysia.

A. Central Plaza

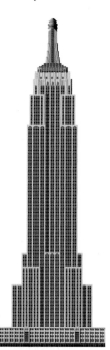

B. Empire State Building

3. A star of the New York skyline and of a popular movie, *King Kong,* this building became the world's tallest in 1931. It rises 1,250 feet (381 meters) and has 102 floors.

4. This tower in Hong Kong has 78 stories and is 1,227 feet (374 meters) tall. Completed in 1992, it is now among the tallest buildings in the world.

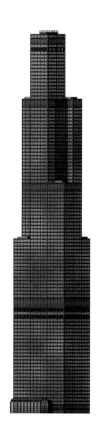

C. Sears Tower

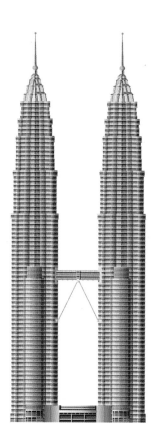

D. Petronas Towers

Are There Other Amazing Buildings?

Some buildings are so amazing that they have become as famous as the people who designed them. Here are some examples of famous buildings and their designers.

Have you ever seen a building that looked like a golf ball? American designer Buckminster Fuller built one. It's called a geodesic (jee oh DEHS ihk) dome. Fuller wanted to express the needs of modern life in his buildings. His building was a large, lightweight structure that could be built quickly or taken down quickly.

The geodesic dome in Montreal, Canada, was designed by Buckminster Fuller.

Some buildings have familiar shapes such as squares, rectangles, and triangles. One structure, the entrance to the Louvre museum in Paris, France, looks like

a large glass pyramid. It was designed by Chinese American architect I. M. Pei.

Some homes may look like castles, but others look like they are part of the scenery. American architect Frank Lloyd Wright became known for building homes that seemed to grow out of the ground. He used earthy-brown colors and materials such as wood to make the houses seem to be part of nature.

The entrance to the Louvre museum in Paris looks like a giant glass pyramid.

Frank Lloyd Wright designed homes that blend with their surroundings.

Many architects have copied a house built around 1930 by French architect Le Corbusier. It is called the Villa Savoye, in Poissy, France. It is made of white concrete, stands on stilts, has a flat roof, and walls of windows.

What Are Some Natural Wonders?

Many of the world's most amazing sights were not made by people. Nature has some of the best attractions.

Some of the most beautiful natural wonders on Earth feature spectacular rivers or waterfalls. For instance, the Amazon River in South America is so wide that in some places you can't see the other side. It is the second longest river in the world. The Amazon starts in Peru and flows all the way across Brazil to the Atlantic Ocean.

Amazon River

Tourists walk along a catwalk (elevated walkway) on the Brazil side of Iguaçu Falls.

Also in South America are the Iguaçu Falls. This is actually an entire system of nearly 500 waterfalls that are separated by small islands. The falls form part of the border between Argentina and Brazil. The site is one of the most popular attractions in South America.

Wide beams of colored light shine on rushing, falling, crashing water at Niagara Falls. Niagara Falls is made up of two waterfalls, the Horseshoe Falls on the Canadian side of the border and the American Falls on the U.S. side. Millions of people visit this site each year.

The Niagara Falls crash into a canyon between the United States, *left*, and Canada, *right*.

Victoria Falls, Africa

In Africa, the rushing waters of the Victoria Falls, on the border of Zambia and Zimbabwe, sound like thunder. The fall's huge clouds of spray look like thick white smoke. At its highest point, this waterfall on the Zambezi River plunges 355 feet (110 meters) into a rocky canyon.

The world's largest desert is also a natural wonder. This desert, the Sahara, also lies in the continent of Africa. The Sahara is almost the size of the entire United States. Part of this desert is sand, but most of it is rock and gravel plains.

The Sahara, in Africa, has huge sand dunes and rock formations.

Sometimes, it's not the place that's a natural wonder—but what lives there. Tsavo (SAH voh) National Park in Kenya stretches for thousands of miles. But the wondrous part of the park is the animals—buffaloes, cheetahs, elephants, rhinoceroses, and zebras, for instance—that roam freely there.

Tsavo National Park, Africa

With some wonders, it is the actual site that's amazing. In North America, the Colorado River has been cutting a giant canyon in Arizona for 6 million years. This valley is so deep that people call it the Grand Canyon. In some places, the canyon is 1 mile (1.6 kilometers) deep and up to 18 miles (29 kilometers) wide.

Grand Canyon, North America

The Great Barrier Reef, in Australia, is home to an amazing variety of fish.

Some natural wonders are underwater! A coral reef is made up of the hardened skeletons of tiny animals called coral polyps. The Great Barrier Reef, off the coast of Australia, is the largest coral reef in the world. This chain of reefs extends for about 1,400 miles (2,300 kilometers). People from all over the world come to see the amazing variety of fish that live there.

Mount Fuji is a sacred place to many Japanese people.

Mount Everest, in Asia, is the highest mountain in the world.

Some natural wonders are mountains. Mount Fuji is the pride of Japan and is sacred to many Japanese people.

The highest mountain in the world is also in Asia. Mount Everest, on the borders of Tibet and Nepal, is 29,035 feet (8,850 meters) high. Everest is called Chomolungma by the Tibetans and Sagarmatha by the Nepalese, both names basically mean "Goddess Mother of the Earth." Many Buddhists—followers of a major religion founded about 500 B.C. by a teacher who came to be known as Buddha—consider Mount Everest to be sacred.

The Dome of the Rock, in Israel, is sacred to Muslims.

Where Do People Worship?

For thousands of years, people have built places for prayer and worship. Jews build **synagogues** (SIHN uh gahgs). Muslims build **mosques** (mahsks). Christians build churches. Buddhists build temples.

The city of Jerusalem in Israel is sacred to Jews, Christians, and Muslims. The Western Wall is sacred to Jews because it is all that is left of their ancient holy temple. Jews come from all over the world to pray there. The wall is also called the Wailing Wall because Jews go there to recall their sufferings.

Near the Western Wall stands the Dome of the Rock. This building is sacred to Muslims because it covers the spot from which they believe the Prophet Muhammad rose to heaven.

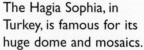

Many Jews worship at the Western Wall, in Israel.

A remarkable church is the Hagia Sophia (HAY ee uh soh FEE uh), built from 532 to 537 as a cathedral in Constantinople (kahn stan tihn OH puhl) (now Istanbul), Turkey. It now serves as a museum. Inside, many walls are lined with marble and beautiful mosaics.

The Hagia Sophia, in Turkey, is famous for its huge dome and mosaics.

Muslims from all over the world travel to the Great Mosque in Saudi Arabia.

The center of worship for all Muslims, or followers of Islam, is the Great Mosque in Mecca, Saudi Arabia. In the courtyard of the Great Mosque is a small building shaped like a box, called the Kaaba (KAH buh). The Kaaba holds the sacred Black Stone that Muslims believe God sent

Many people come to see the amazing Angkor Wat in Cambodia.

124

from heaven. Muslims face in the direction of the Kaaba when they pray.

Hindus in India consider a river sacred. Each year, thousands of Hindus visit such cities as Varanasi (vuh RAH nuh see) and Allahabad (AL uh huh BAD) to bathe in the Ganges River and take home some of its water. Hindus believe that bathing in the Ganges cleanses the body and spirit.

Saint Peter's Basilica in Rome has this beautiful dome.

A world center for Roman Catholic people is Vatican City, which is located in Rome. Saint Peter's Basilica, also called St. Peter's Church, is there. Its beautiful dome was designed by the great Italian artist Michelangelo.

The outside of the pyramid-shaped Angkor Wat (ANG kohr WAHT) in Cambodia has richly carved sandstone and sculptured columns. The temple was built in the 1100's to honor the Hindu god Vishnu.

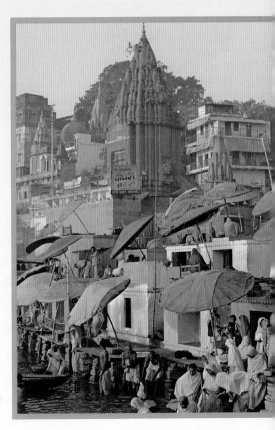

In India, Hindus bathe in the Ganges River.

How Do You Find Your Way?

How can you find the elephants at the zoo?

How did pirates find buried treasure?

How can you find the ice-cream store in a huge mall?

How can you help your friends find their way to your house?

How can you find your way around a strange city?

It's easy. Use a map!

Maps are important for anyone who is traveling or exploring and for people who are just curious about the world. They help you find your way around strange places, and they are great fun to use—once you know how!

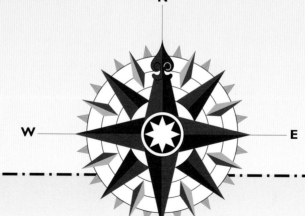

Bay of Biscay

La Coruña

Gijón

Cantabrian Mts.

Bilbao

Vigo

Pyre

Ebro

Porto

Valladolid

Duero

Saragossa

RTUGAL

Madrid

oon

Tagus

SPAIN

Guadiana

Córdoba

Mur

Seville

Granada

Atlantic
Ocean

Sierra Nevada

Málaga

Mediterr

Strait of Gibraltar

Gibraltar
(U.K.)

Tangier

Oran

MOROCCO

Rabat

Fez

127

Casablanca

Pictures of the Earth

A map is a kind of picture of Earth. Maps can show the whole Earth, or just parts of it. There are maps of the world, maps of countries, maps of cities, and maps of neighborhoods.

10°
Bay of Biscay
La Coruña
Gijón
Cantabrian Mts.
Bilbao
Bordeaux
FRANCE
Toulouse
Vigo
Pyrenees
ANDORRA
Porto
Valladolid
Duero
Saragossa
40°
PORTUGAL
Madrid
Barcelona
Lisbon
S P A I N
Valencia
Guadiana
Balearic Is.
Córdoba
Seville
Murcia
Granada
Atlantic
Ocean
Sierra Nevada
Mediterranean Sea
Málaga
Algiers
Strait of Gibraltar
Gibraltar
(U.K.)
Tangier
Oran
Chelif
MOROCCO
Rabat
ALGERIA
Fez
Casablanca
0°

terrain map

There are also maps of the moon, maps of the land under the oceans, maps of almost any place you can think of. Zoos, national parks, shopping malls, and other places often have maps to help people find their way around. Even though maps can show all of these things, many are still small enough to fit in your backpack!

The earth has tall mountains, deep valleys, winding rivers, and vast oceans, yet maps make the earth look flat. They are drawn as if you are high up, looking straight down on the land. By looking at a map, you can see what lies beyond a forest or on the other side of a mountain.

Looking at a map also tells you whether something is north, south, east, or west of other areas on the map. When you are trying to find a place, such as your friend's house across town or the bathroom in the shopping mall, you have to know in which direction to walk.

There are many kinds of maps. A map that shows how rough or smooth the land is is called a physical or **terrain**

road map

map. It uses color to show mountains, rivers, plains, valleys, and other features.

A road map shows streets, roads, and highways. Some road maps show only the main roads, but others show small roads, too.

A product map shows all the things that are made and grown in an area. A **population** map shows how many people live in different parts of a country. A weather map shows the weather in an area. A historical map shows the world as it was long ago, or how

product map

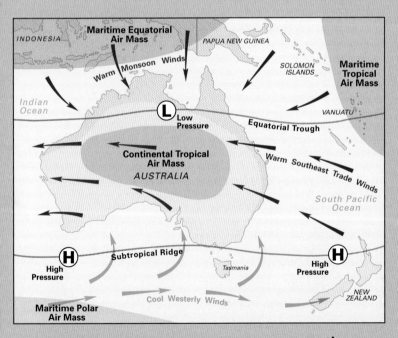

weather map

people thought the world looked at that time.

A **chart** is a kind of map used by sailors and airplane pilots. It shows features of the oceans and skies.

Sailors and pilots use a chart, along with special instruments, to find their way.

How Maps Help Us

Now you know about some different kinds of maps. Who do you think would use these maps? Why would they use them?

1. When would someone need a road map?

2. Why would a person want to know what products are made or grown in a state or country?

3. Who would want to know weather in different parts of the country or world?

4. Why would someone need a map of a shopping mall?

TRY THIS!
2

Answers: 1. A person driving a car in a strange place would need a road map to keep from getting lost. 2. A person thinking about moving to another state or country might want to know what kinds of jobs there were. 3. Business travelers and people going on vacation would want to know the weather where they are going. 4. Mall maps help people find stores, restaurants, and bathrooms.

How Maps Work

Your friend wants to visit you but does not know how to get to your house. You want to help her find it. You could tell her your street address, but that wouldn't help if she didn't know where the street was. You might give her a picture of your house. That would tell her what your house looked like, but it wouldn't show her how to find it. Well, how can you help her? You could draw a map!

Why is a map better than a picture for finding your way somewhere? See for yourself! Here is a picture of a neighborhood. It was taken from an

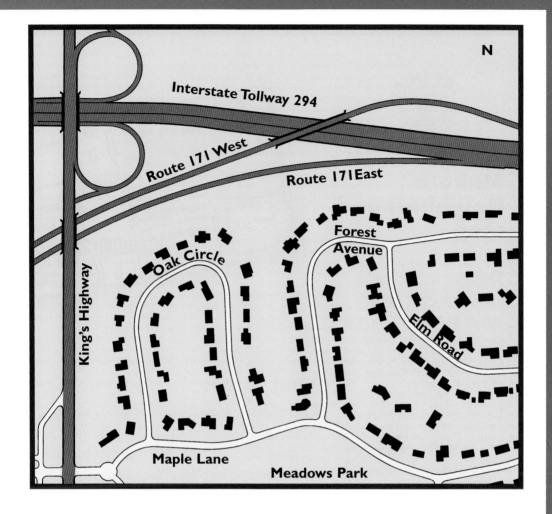

airplane. What do you see in the picture?
Can you find houses, trees, and roads?
What else do you see? Would a picture like
this of your neighborhood help your friend
find your house?

Now look at the map of the neighborhood.
Can you find the houses and roads? What
does the map tell you that the picture does
not?

TRY THIS!
2

Make a Neighborhood Map

One way to help your friend find your house quickly and easily is to draw a map. It's easy to make a map of your neighborhood, and it's fun, too.

You Will Need:

plain white paper
pencils
a ruler
crayons or markers
tracing paper

What To Do:

1. First, walk around your neighborhood and make a list of the things you want to show on your map. You may want to ask an adult to help you. You might want to show your house, a friend's house, the park, or your school. Think about where places are, how far apart they are, and what shape they are. As you walk, write down the names of the streets in the order in which you get to them. Which buildings and streets would help someone find your house?

2. Next, draw your map. Draw the streets in pencil and show where they cross. Print the name of each street on your map.

Then add shapes that stand for your
friend's house, a mailbox, or a store. You
might also need to add streets that aren't
on the map. Label each street. Then add
labels for important places such as your
home and school.

3. Now color your map. Use different colors
for such areas as houses, streets, and parks.
At the bottom of the map, list what each
color stands for.

To find out whether your map works, let
a friend use it to try to find your house or
another place on your map.

How Do You Read a Map?

Maps can give you lots of information about exciting places, if you know how to read them. To read a map, you have to understand "map language."

Map language is made up of names, numbers, colors, shapes, lines, and tiny pictures called **symbols**. These names, numbers, and symbols stand for the things you might look for on a map, such as cities, rivers, or roads. Most maps also have a map legend. A map legend explains what the symbols and colors on a map mean.

A map can help you plan a family vacation.

An important word in map language is **direction.** The most important directions to know are north, south, east, and west.

North is the direction that leads to the North Pole. South is the opposite. It faces the South Pole. East is where the sun rises and west is where the sun sets.

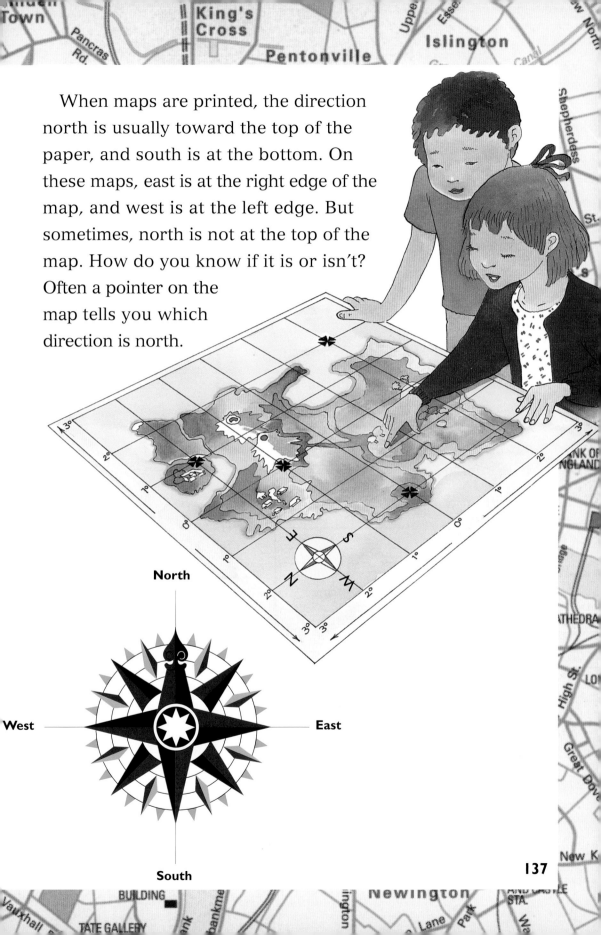

When maps are printed, the direction north is usually toward the top of the paper, and south is at the bottom. On these maps, east is at the right edge of the map, and west is at the left edge. But sometimes, north is not at the top of the map. How do you know if it is or isn't? Often a pointer on the map tells you which direction is north.

North

West

East

South

137

Understanding Map Symbols

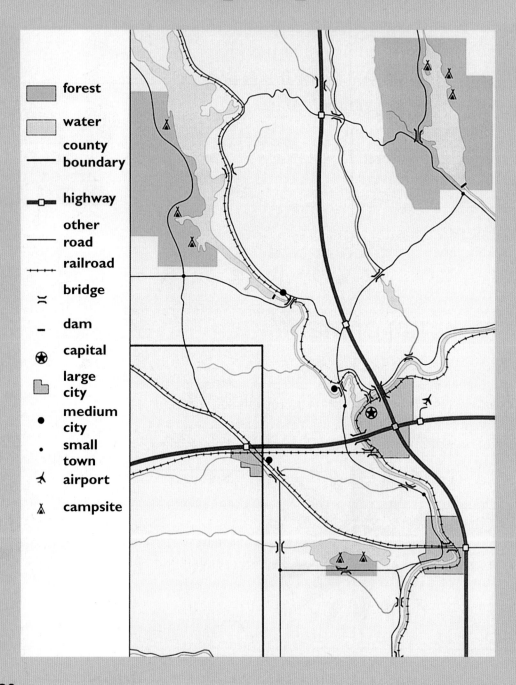

forest

water

county boundary

highway

other road

railroad

bridge

dam

capital

large city

medium city

small town

airport

campsite

When you walk to the park, you might see trees, grass, flowers, and buildings. You won't see these things on a map, but the map will still help you find out where the park is. How does it do this? With symbols.

Map symbols stand for real things on the surface of the earth. The map legend shows what the symbols mean. The colors help, too. Highways are usually shown as red or black lines. The wider the line, the bigger the highway. Crossed black lines stand for railroad tracks, and a small black dot stands for a city. A star or dot inside a circle means a capital city. To find an airport, look for a tiny airplane on the map.

Water is shown in blue, so squiggly blue lines show rivers. Sometimes color is used to show the height of the land. Low land may be green. High mountains may be dark brown.

The next time you see a map, take a close look at it. You'll be surprised to find how much a small map can show.

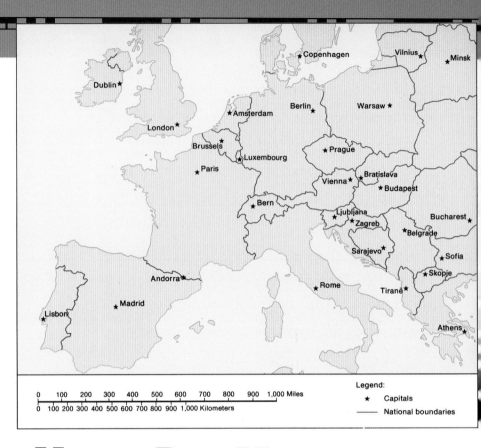

Legend:
★   Capitals
——   National boundaries

How Do You Measure Distance?

If you are using a map to get to your friend's house, you can figure out how far you have to travel. First, you have to learn something about distance. The word *distance* means the space between things.

A map has to show distance much smaller than it actually is. So, at the top or bottom of most maps, you will see what looks like a ruler. This is called the **map scale**. The scale shows what the distance on a map equals in real distance.

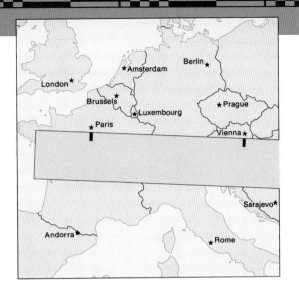

The scale shown on the previous page is a straight line on which distances are marked.

Each mark stands for a certain number of miles or kilometers. To find the real distance between two places, you first measure the distance between them on the map. To do this, line up the two places on the edge of a piece of paper. Make a mark for each place. Then, move the paper down to the scale. Line up one mark with the 0 on the scale. Then read the number that lines up with the other mark.

TRY THIS!
1

To measure distance on a winding road on a map, place a string along the route you want to take. Let the string curve along the curves of the road. Then straighten the string and measure its length on the map scale. The number you get will be the total distance.

Large Scale or Small Scale?

On a map, real land and real oceans are made small enough to fit on paper. The scale of a map is the difference between the map size and the real size. When a map is drawn to scale, everything is made smaller by the same amount.

A large-scale map shows a small area with lots of details. It is what you would see if you were looking down on an area from very close. The highways, streets, parks, and buildings would look large.

A small-scale map shows a large area with not many details. It is what you would see if you were looking down on an area from very far away. You might see main roads, large towns, and rivers or

This large-scale map shows some of Tokyo's important buildings.

Jikei Medical University Hospital

TOKYO

Shiba Post Office

Shiba Public Health Center

Dai-Tokyo Credit Bank

Sakuragawa Primary School

Shiba Fire Station

Onarimon Sta.

Atago Police Station

Shiba Credit Bank

Shiba Park

Japanese Red Cross

Shiba Park Hotel

Shinmei Primary School

200 Yards

200 Meters

mountains. The roads and towns would look small.

The maps on these pages show the same place drawn in different scales. All the maps have useful information. Which map tells you how many towns are near the shore? Which map tells you the main roads in the area? Which map tells you how far it is from the school to the post office?

This small-scale map tells you that Tokyo lies in east-central Japan.

This medium-scale map shows the cities that lie close to Tokyo.

Draw a Map to Scale

You don't need rulers or tape measures to draw a map to scale. Make different maps of your own room—using just your feet!

You Will Need:

graph paper
crayons or markers
a ruler

What To Do:

1. Select two things in your room, such as your dresser and bed, or the door and the window.

2. Estimate, or guess, the distance between the two objects you have chosen.

3. Now use steps to measure the distance. Walk in a straight line, placing your feet from heel to toe. Count how many steps it takes to get from one object to the other. Write down that measurement.

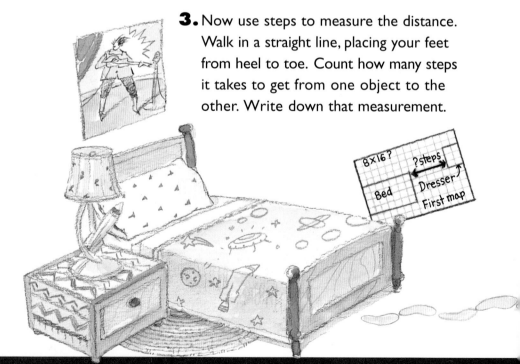

8×16? ?steps Dresser
Bed First map

4. Decide on a scale, such as the length of one square of graph paper equals one step. Draw a map of your room using the measurements (in steps) you just took. Use your scale to show the distance between the two things you chose. At the top or bottom of the map, mark the map scale.

5. Now draw more maps to different scales. For example, one step equals two squares.

6. Give each of your maps a title, such as "first map," "second map," and "third map."

Now you are ready to compare your maps. How are they alike? How are they different?

What Is a Compass?

If you are standing in your front yard, how do you know which way is east? If it's a sunny early morning, you can easily tell. The sun rises in the east, so you just have to face the direction of the rising sun. But what if it is cloudy outside?

Even on a cloudy day, a good way to tell direction is with a **compass.** A simple compass has a magnetized needle that's mounted so that it can turn freely. No matter which way you face or turn the compass, the needle will continue pointing north.

How does a compass tell which way is north? The needle of a compass is a magnet. It points north because it is pulled by a larger magnet—the earth. One end of the earth's magnet is near the North Pole, and the other end is near the South Pole. The north-seeking end of a magnetic needle always points toward the earth's north magnetic pole.

Underneath a compass's needle are the words *north, south, east,* and *west,* or the letters *N, S, E,* and *W.* When you turn the compass so that the needle points to the word *north* or the letter *N,* it is in the right position to show which way is east, west, or south.

Make a Compass

TRY THIS! 2

See for yourself how the north-seeking end of a magnetic needle always points toward the earth's north magnetic pole.

What To Do:

1. Ask an adult to help you rub one end of the needle along the magnet about 12 times. Rub in one direction only and lift the pin up each time. Then place the needle on the cork.

2. Gently place the cork in the bowl of water. At first, the needle and cork will swing around. Then the needle will point steadily in one direction. It points along the line between the earth's magnetic North and South poles. Ask an adult to tell you which end points north.

You Will Need:

a magnet
a straight pin or
  needle
a piece of cork about
  1 in. (2.5 cm) wide by
  1/4 in. (0.6 cm) thick
a bowl of water

To test your compass, walk to different places around your house or in your yard. Does your compass point to the north all the time?

What Does a Globe Show?

Do you like globes? Great! But don't throw away all your maps just yet. Globes are not very easy to carry when you are on a hike or traveling in a car. And they don't show close-up views of places, either.

The earth looks like a big, blue marble to astronauts in outer space. It's easy for them to see the round shape of the earth because they are so far away from it. If you want to see the whole earth at one time, you might look at a map. But mapmakers must squeeze and stretch parts of the world so that they can draw them on a flat map. That means a flat map does not show the true shape of the earth.

A **globe** is a round model of the earth. Globes show the size, shape, and location of land and oceans. Many globes show the boundaries of different

If you want to see the shape of the earth
and you don't have a spaceship, use a globe!

countries. Some globes show how the
mountains, hills, valleys, and oceans
would appear from the sky.

Do you know why most globes are
tilted on their stands? It is because the
earth really is tilted. It spins at a tilt as it
travels around the sun. With a globe, you
see part of the earth at one time. To see
places on the other side, you just turn
the globe.

What Is the Equator?

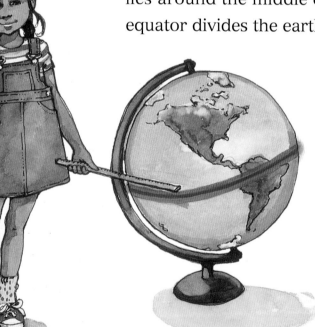

Maps and globes have all kinds of signs and symbols. Often they have certain lines, too. Nearly every map and globe of the world has one very important line. It's called the equator.

An imaginary line called the equator lies around the middle of the earth. The equator divides the earth into the Northern and Southern hemispheres, or halves. The word *hemisphere* means "half of a sphere or ball."

North of the equator is an imaginary line called the Tropic of Cancer. South of the equator is another line called the Tropic of Capricorn. Both lines are named for groups of stars. The areas between the equator and these

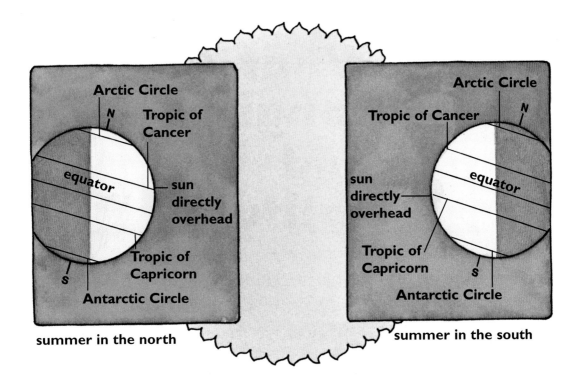

summer in the north

summer in the south

two lines are called the tropics. Once a year the sun is directly over the Tropic of Cancer. That marks the first day of summer in the Northern Hemisphere. Once a year, the sun is directly over the Tropic of Capricorn. That marks the first day of summer in the Southern Hemisphere.

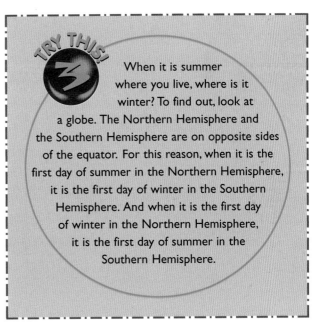

TRY THIS!

When it is summer where you live, where is it winter? To find out, look at a globe. The Northern Hemisphere and the Southern Hemisphere are on opposite sides of the equator. For this reason, when it is the first day of summer in the Northern Hemisphere, it is the first day of winter in the Southern Hemisphere. And when it is the first day of winter in the Northern Hemisphere, it is the first day of summer in the Southern Hemisphere.

What Are Longitude and Latitude?

Look at a globe or a map of the world. Have you ever wondered why they have so many lines? There are no lines on the earth, so why are there lines on globes and maps?

On a map, the prime meridian passes through Greenwich, England.

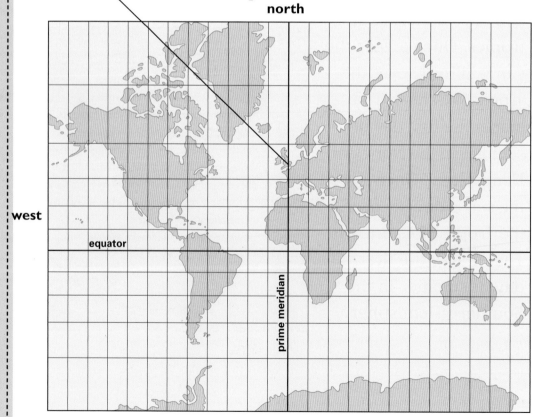

Greenwich

north

west

east

equator

prime meridian

south

The lines help people find places. The lines are something like city streets. When two friends meet at a corner, they are meeting where two streets cross. On a globe or map, the east-west lines cross the north-south lines. Every place can be found on a map by looking near where two of the lines cross.

parallels of latitude

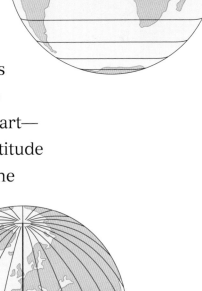

The east-west lines measure how far north or how far south a place is from the equator. This measurement is called latitude. Because the lines are parallel—always the same distance apart— they are called parallels of latitude. Latitude is measured in units called degrees. The symbol ° after each number is a degree sign. Latitude is always given as so many degrees north or south of the equator. The equator is 0° latitude.

The north-south lines measure distance east and west, or longitude. These lines are called meridians. A line called the prime meridian is 0° longitude. All other meridians are measured as so many degrees east or west of this line.

meridians

Find the Buried Treasure

Have you ever wanted to hunt for buried treasure? You can do just that with this buried treasure map. Read a clue below. Then use the longitude and latitude to find the place of each hidden treasure on the map. Write the name of the place where you find each treasure on a piece of paper. *Check your answers against those on page 155.*

You Will Need:

paper
a pencil or pen

1. sunken treasure ship, latitude 2° north, longitude 2° east.

2. buried chest, latitude 2° south, longitude 0°.

3. ancient jars, latitude 0° north, longitude 2° east.

4. silver cups, latitude 1° north, longitude 2° west.

5. old musical instruments, latitude 2° south, longitude 2° east.

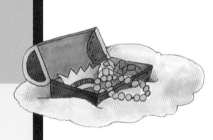

6. ancient carvings, latitude 0°, longitude 1° west.

7. another sunken treasure, latitude 1° north, longitude 1° east.

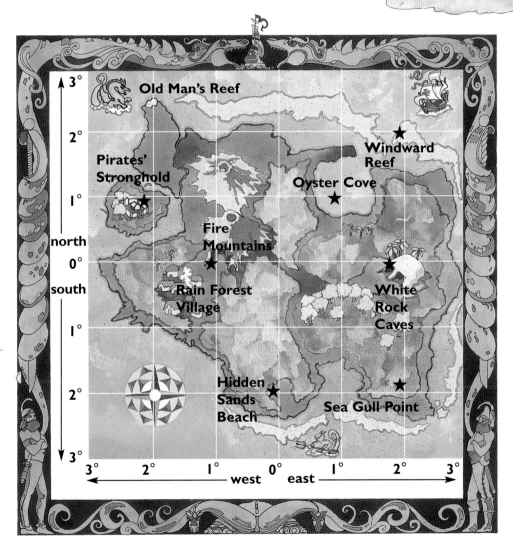

3° Old Man's Reef

2° Windward Reef

Pirates' Stronghold

Oyster Cove

1°

north

Fire Mountains

0°

south

Rain Forest Village

White Rock Caves

1°

2° Hidden Sands Beach   Sea Gull Point

3°

3° 2° 1° 0° 1° 2° 3°

west ← → east

Maps of Long Ago

People have used maps for thousands of years. The earliest maps probably were simply scratches in the dirt. Early people made these scratches to show where to find water, food, or their caves. Later, people used nearby materials to make maps. Early Chinese people carved maps of their empire into bamboo or stone or painted them on rolls of silk. Certain people of the Pacific Islands mapped out their region with palm sticks and shells.

Long ago, in the Middle Ages, some people thought the earth was flat. They believed you could fall off the edge of the world if you sailed too far out to sea. Explorers such as Christopher Columbus and Ferdinand Magellan changed these ideas. They collected information about countries outside Europe for European mapmakers.

KNOW It All!

The earliest known map is a clay tablet found in Iraq. It was made more than 4,000 years ago. It shows settlements, waterways, and mountains.

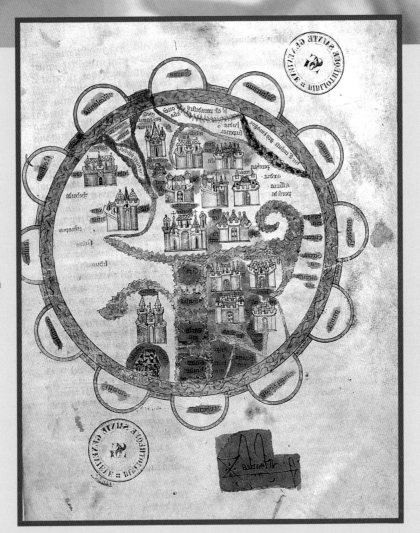

a map more than 700 years old

When hot-air balloons were invented in the 1780's and airplanes in the 1900's, people finally got a bird's-eye view of the world. This helped them to make better maps.

Today, we use computers and photographs taken from airplanes and satellites to make maps of the world. We can even make maps for areas that nobody can get to.

Mapmakers

This surveyor in Hawaii uses a special instrument to measure the area where a building will go.

There are many different kinds of maps and many different jobs for people who help create them. Let's take a look at some of the people who help make maps.

A person called a **surveyor** (suhr VAY uhr) uses special instruments to measure distances, angles, and heights to figure out where a place is and how big it is. Surveyors measure and record the positions of things and the shape of the earth's surface.

Some people photograph the land from an airplane. The aerial photographs are used by people called **photogrammetrists** (FOH toh GRAM uh trihsts) to measure land areas, lakes,

This photograph of the Allard River in Quebec, Canada, was taken from the air and can be used to make a map.

Cartographers make many of today's maps on computers.

and other features of the earth. The photographs show wide areas of land and can give much more information than a person could gather while on the ground.

Cartographers (kahr TAHG ruh fuhrz) use information from surveyors and photogrammetrists to make maps. Many cartographers use computers to draw an actual map. They add symbols and colors to help people understand all of the different kinds of information on a map.

A **geographer** (jee AHG ruh fuhr) studies how people and animals relate to the land. Some geographers study the places where people live. Others study the resources people use, such as water, land, and oil. Still others study rivers, mountains, and oceans. They put all of the information they find on maps to show other people.

Taking a Trip

Before you take a trip, there is so much to do! It helps to be prepared, whether you are going on a weekend campout, a week-long visit to a relative's house, or a two-week vacation to another country. Even on the most carefully planned trips, there are changes and surprises. That is part of what makes travel interesting!

What's Your Favorite Place?

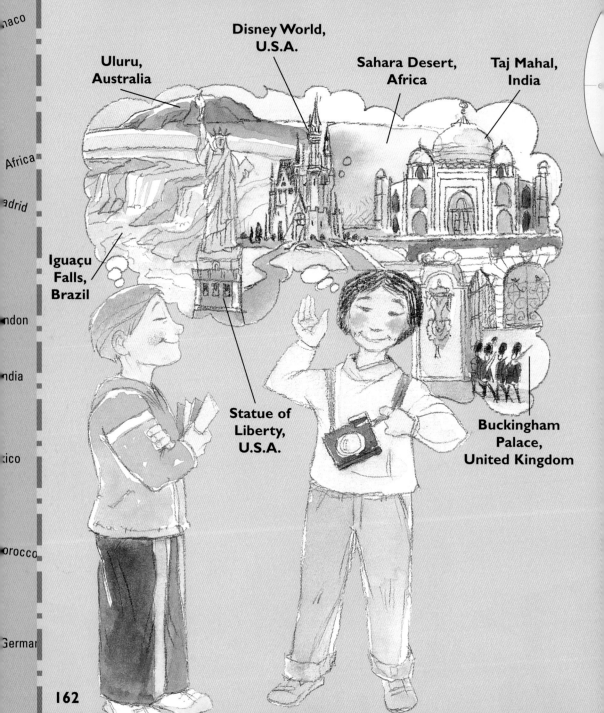

Uluru,
Australia

Disney World,
U.S.A.

Sahara Desert,
Africa

Taj Mahal,
India

Iguaçu
Falls,
Brazil

Statue of
Liberty,
U.S.A.

Buckingham
Palace,
United Kingdom

162

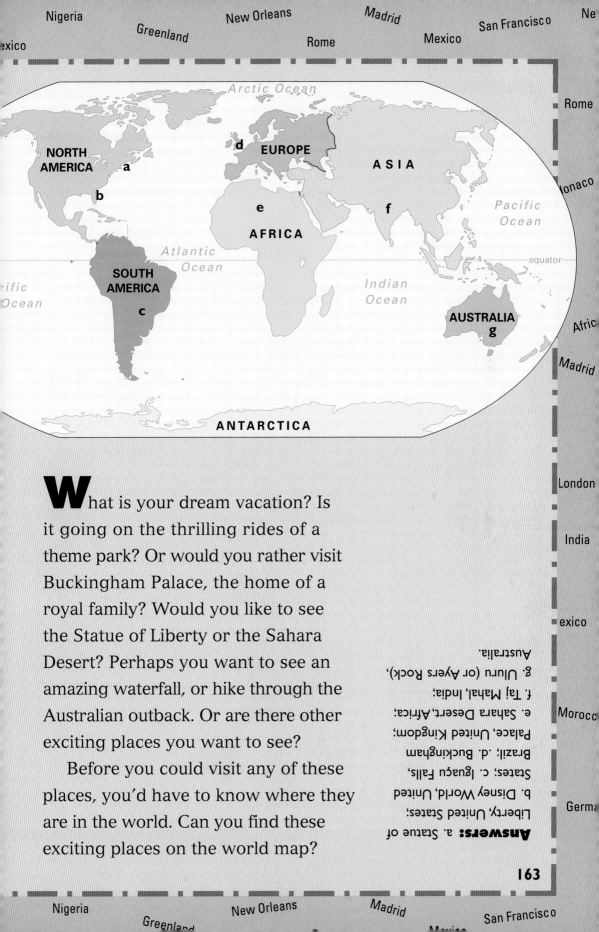

Arctic Ocean

NORTH AMERICA

a

b

EUROPE

d

ASIA

e

AFRICA

f

Pacific Ocean

Atlantic Ocean

SOUTH AMERICA

c

Indian Ocean

equator

AUSTRALIA

g

ANTARCTICA

What is your dream vacation? Is it going on the thrilling rides of a theme park? Or would you rather visit Buckingham Palace, the home of a royal family? Would you like to see the Statue of Liberty or the Sahara Desert? Perhaps you want to see an amazing waterfall, or hike through the Australian outback. Or are there other exciting places you want to see?

Before you could visit any of these places, you'd have to know where they are in the world. Can you find these exciting places on the world map?

Answers: a. Statue of Liberty, United States; b. Disney World, United States; c. Iguaçu Falls, Brazil; d. Buckingham Palace, United Kingdom; e. Sahara Desert, Africa; f. Taj Mahal, India; g. Uluru (or Ayers Rock), Australia.

Planning Your Vacation

The more you know about where you are going, the more prepared you will be once you get there. Planning ahead helps you remember to pack the things you need. And it helps you avoid disappointments, too. How will you feel if you find out that the museum is closed on Monday—the day you're there?!

Making a to-do list can sometimes help you plan a trip. The travelers below are going on very different trips. Each one has to make a plan to prepare for the trip. Can you match each traveler with a to-do list?

Henry is planning a week-long trip to his grandmother's house.

Joe is taking a day trip to the beach.

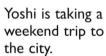

Yoshi is taking a weekend trip to the city.

To-Do List 1

- Bring lots of snacks and cold drinks.
- Pack sunscreen and beach cover-up.
- Don't forget the towels!
- Find out if it's OK to use inflatable rafts or beach balls.

To-Do List 2

- Pack enough jeans, shirts, socks, and underwear.
- Bring favorite stuffed animal and book.
- Pack camera.
- Pack notebook for jotting down stories.

To-Do List 3

- Get a visitor's map.
- Bring money for **souvenirs** and entrance fees. Don't forget change for the bus!
- Check out must-see places to visit and find out when they are open.

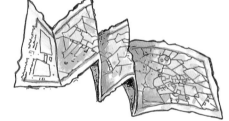

Do you want to take a trip somewhere new?
Get the facts about new places before you go:

- Head to your local library. Check out books about the history and the people in the area you plan to visit. Find stories set in that area, too.
- Ask permission to check the Internet to find the Web sites of tourist bureaus or chambers of commerce.
- Write to organizations to request maps and calendars of events.

Answers: Henry, list 2; Joe, list 1; Yoshi, list 3.

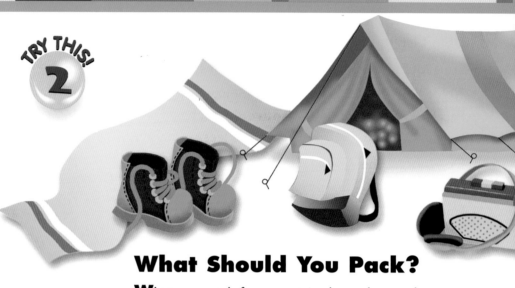

What Should You Pack?

What you pack for your trip depends on where you are going, how long you will be there, and what your interests are. You also need to think about what the weather will be like! Don't stuff your suitcase too full, though. It will be too heavy. You might want to bring along a backpack for day trips or the plane ride.

It's a warm summer day. Mia, Rob, and Jake have planned very different vacations, and they don't know what to pack! Mia is going camping, Rob is going sightseeing in the city, and Jake is going to the seashore. Take a look at the list and choose which things Mia, Rob, and Jake should put in their suitcase.

Some items will be needed by more than one person. Other items won't be needed at all.

See answers on page 167.

- beach towel
- snowshoes
- small radio with earphones
- visitor's map
- sandals
- camera and film
- hiking boots
- coins for the bus
- tent and sleeping bag
- bathing suit
- cup, plate, fork, and spoon
- bug spray
- flashlight
- sunscreen
- toothbrush and soap
- parka

167

Never a Dull Moment

Part of your vacation will be spent standing in line. You may have to stand in line to board a plane, get a table at a restaurant, or ride a roller coaster. Here's how you can keep busy while you wait:

- Play an alphabet game. With a friend or a brother or sister, take turns finding things that begin with A, then B, then C, and so on.

- Guess the mood of other people in line. What does their **body language** tell you? What do their facial expressions say? Are they tired? Bored? Excited?

- Make a count. How many people in line are wearing sunglasses? How many have backpacks? How many children are under the age of 6? How many people are over 70?

- Read, read, read. Read a brochure, guidebook, or map about the place you are visiting. If you're at a restaurant, read the menu. Then you'll know what you want to eat before you sit down. If you are at an amusement park, read the safety rules or study the park map to decide what you want to do next!

TRY THIS! 1

Did you pack your gorilla? Here's a fun game for two or more people to play on a long ride. Players take turns adding silly objects to their suitcases, trying to remember them all in the correct order. Older kids might want to list the contents of their suitcase in alphabetical order. For example, **Person 1:** "I'm going on a trip, and I'm going to pack my gorilla."

Person 2: "I'm going on a trip, and I'm going to pack my gorilla and a peanut butter sandwich."

Person 3: "I'm going on a trip, and I'm going to pack my gorilla, a peanut butter sandwich, and a snowman. . . ."

Keep this up until a player forgets an item. Then that player is out of the game. The winner is the last person remaining.

Are You a Savvy Traveler?

The word *savvy* (SAV ee) means "smart." Smart travelers are ready for new sights, new sounds, new tastes, and new experiences. They respect other people's languages, customs, and foods, even though they might seem strange at first. Savvy travelers expect surprises, and they know that each journey is a chance to learn something new.

Take this quiz to find out if you are a savvy traveler. You can pick more than one letter for each number. Then count the number of a's, b's, c's, and d's you score. *See what your score means on page 173.*

1. You are taking a stroll down a wooded path. You spot a flower you've never seen before. You:

a. pick the flower so no one else will find it.

b. ignore the flower. Woods are boring!

c. look up the flower in your nature guide and make a sketch of it in your notebook.

d. have a contest to see how many unusual flowers you can find.

2. It is late afternoon in a Spanish village. All the stores and restaurants are closed for **siesta.** You:

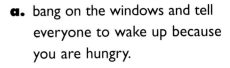

a. bang on the windows and tell everyone to wake up because you are hungry.

b. pout in your hotel room.

c. use the time to read about local customs.

d. have a picnic in the park with the snacks you packed in your backpack.

3. It is your only day to go to the beach. Suddenly, it starts to rain. You:

a. tell everyone that your trip is ruined and you want to go home.

b. sit in your room all day and watch it rain.

c. use the time to write postcards to your friends.

d. check out a museum you hadn't planned to visit.

4. You are in a restaurant and the waiter brings you an odd-looking dish you've never had before. You:

a. pinch your nose and yell "Gross!"

b. push the plate away from you when no one is looking.

c. ask the waiter to tell you the name of the dish and how to pronounce it.

d. try the dish even though you don't know whether you will like it.

Mostly A's:
Tourist, go home! You won't enjoy your trip, and you may keep other people from enjoying theirs.

Mostly B's:
B is for boring. You need to put more effort into your travels if you want to have fun!

Mostly C's:
Your willingness to learn about the places you visit makes you a savvy traveler.

Mostly D's:
You're savvy, too. Your adventurous spirit guarantees that you will have fun wherever you go.

5. Your parents tell you that you are going to an art museum instead of the amusement park. You:

a. plan to bring your in-line skates so you can play tag with your sister.

b. sigh loudly and dawdle behind your parents once you get there.

c. take the museum tour and learn about the paintings.

d. go on an art museum treasure hunt.

Make the Memories Last and Last

While you are on vacation, you can do things that will help you remember your trip when you return home.

• Snap Away—Photographs are sometimes better than postcards. Photos are a record of things you have actually seen. Be sure your camera has plenty of film and batteries. You have to take lots of pictures to get a few great ones.

• Write a Note to Yourself—Mail yourself a postcard every day. You will have pictures that you couldn't take by yourself, and you'll have a daily record of your thoughts and adventures.

• Start a Collection—Keep menus, maps, and ticket stubs for your scrapbook. You might want to buy one or two souvenirs, such as a T-shirt or key chain with the name of the place you visited. But don't overdo it—you'll have to carry them all home!

• Share and Remember—Once you are home, it is fun

to show off your treasures. It also feels great to eat your favorite snacks and sleep in your own bed again. Traveling gives you a break from your everyday life, but it also makes you appreciate the things at home!

TRY THIS!
1

Start a postcard collection. Collect them when you travel, and save the ones that people send you. By studying postcards from different places, you can learn about their climate, culture, geography, places to visit, money, and even language.

Have you traveled to another country? Maybe you know someone who has. Here's a fun poem by Shel Silverstein about a grandfather who travels around the world and sends back all kinds of surprises.

Surprise!

My Grandpa went to Myrtle Beach
And sent us back a turtle each.
And then he went to Katmandu
And mailed a real live Cockatoo.
From Rio an iguana came,
A smelly goat arrived from Spain.
Now he's in India, you see—
My Grandpa always
    thinks of me.

Do you ever dream of a special place that's all your own? Is the place real or imaginary? Where might that place be? How would you get there? Think about your special place as you read this poem by Walter de la Mare.

Somewhere

Could you tell me the way to Somewhere—
    *Some*where, *Some*where,
    I have heard of a place called Somewhere—
    But know not where it can be.
      It makes no difference,
      Whether or not
      I go in dreams
      Or trudge on foot:
Would you tell me the way to Somewhere,
    The Somewhere meant for me.

Who Helps People Travel?

Would you like to help people travel to exciting places? Then maybe a career in travel is for you! There are many different types of jobs in travel. Someday you may want to have a job like one of these:

Travel agents plan trips. They arrange airline flights and hotel rooms. Travel agents also arrange transportation and sightseeing tours. They tell you when to catch a tour bus or how much the tickets will cost. They find out about fun things to do, places to see, and how to dress for the weather. They also provide maps and tour books to help you plan your trip.

A couple plans a vacation with the help of a travel agent.

With a computer terminal on one side and a phone on the other, **airline reservation desk clerks** help people without a travel agent choose the right flights. They help travelers find flights that cost less or flights with no stops.

At hotels and motels, **front-desk clerks** are responsible for collecting and giving out room keys. They also answer the phone and handle guests' phone messages and mail.

Do you love food? Many fine **chefs** work in hotels, where they prepare fancy meals. Airline chefs prepare meals that are sometimes served on long flights.

The desk clerks at a hotel check in hotel guests and help them during their visit.

Travelers often enjoy delicious meals prepared by trained chefs.

Cruise directors make sure there are many fun activities for passengers to do on the deck of a cruise ship.

Sometimes a travel career means working on water! If you enjoy boating, perhaps the job of **cruise director** is for you. Cruise ships are floating hotels. A cruise director plans fun activities on board the ship as well as on shore. For example, on the ship, people can take dance lessons or exercise classes, play board games, or watch a concert. On shore, people can shop, sightsee, or go to the beach. Chefs on cruise ships prepare delicious feasts for the passengers and get to travel the world at the same time!

Would you love to travel? Then perhaps you would like to be a **flight attendant.** Flight attendants serve food and drinks and help make people comfortable during a flight. They also help keep passengers safe in an emergency.

A flight attendant teaches passengers what to do in case of emergency.

   With lots of training, you could become an **airline pilot.** Pilots figure out a plane's route and give the flight plan to the air-traffic controllers. They check the cockpit controls to make sure the plane is in good working order. Then they carry passengers safely where they want to go.

Airline pilots must pay attention to many controls inside the cockpit so that passengers travel safely.

Be a Travel Agent

Part of a travel agent's job is to create an itinerary (eye TIHN uh REHR ee), a route for your journey. Imagine that you are a travel agent planning a trip for yourself and a friend to an exciting place.

You Will Need:

white paper
a stapler
newspapers and magazines
   that an adult has given you
   permission to cut up
scissors
crayons or markers

What To Do:

1. Decide how many days you and your friend would like to travel. Then staple several sheets of paper together to make a short booklet. Allow two pages for each day of your trip.

2. Look through the newspapers and magazines. Cut out pictures of exciting and interesting places, such as museums, monuments, amusement parks, zoos, and nature parks, that you would like to visit. Remember, you're not really traveling, so anything goes! Also cut out pictures of hotels, motels, campgrounds, and restaurants where you would enjoy staying and eating.

3. Now arrange your pictures so that you have two or three places to visit, one place to stay, and two or three restaurants for each day of your vacation.

4. Glue the pictures into your booklet. You might want to put numbers by each picture to show what you would do first, second, and so on. You also could put the words *breakfast, lunch,* and *dinner* next to the restaurants to show where you would eat each meal.

Now you are ready to present the "itinerary" to your friend. "Bon Voyage!" This is French for "have a good trip!"

Glossary

Here are some of the words you read in this book. Many of them may be new to you. Some are hard to pronounce. But since you will see them again, they are good words to know. Next to each word, you will see how to say it correctly: **population** (PAHP yuh LAY shuhn). The part shown in small capital letters is said a little more loudly than the rest of the word. The part in large capital letters is said the loudest. Under each word are one or two sentences that tell what the word means.

B

bartering (BAR tuhr ihng)
Bartering means swapping one thing for another instead of paying for it with money. Before people worked in jobs that paid money, they used bartering to get the goods they needed.

body language (BAH dee LANG wihj)
Body language is a way of communicating without words. It is made up of movements and facial expressions. You can often tell how a person is feeling by studying their body language.

C

caravan (KAR uh van)
A caravan is a group of people and animals traveling in a long line through open country. Many people who live in deserts travel in caravans.

chart (chahrt)
A chart is a map of the sea or harbor. Sailors use charts to find their way around coasts, rocks, and shallow places.

climate (KLY miht)
The climate of a place is the usual weather it has. The climate in tropical rain forests is hot and steamy.

compass (KUHM puhs)
A compass is an instrument that helps people find directions. A compass is useful when you are hiking in the woods.

continent (KAHN tuh nuhnt)
A continent is a very large area of land, mostly or completely surrounded by oceans. Africa is a continent.

D

direction (duh REHK shuhn)
Direction is the way something is moving or pointing. A map can tell you in which direction something is, whether it is north, south, east, or west. If a person gives directions, he or she is telling how to get somewhere.

distance (DIHS tuhns)
Distance is the space between two things. The distance between two places is often given in miles or kilometers.

drawn to scale (drawn too skayl)
A map is drawn to scale when the size and place of objects pictured on the map are drawn in relation to the size and place of the objects in real life. Many maps of countries and cities are drawn to scale.

E

equator (ih KWAY tuhr)
The equator is an imaginary line around the middle of the Earth, halfway between the North and South poles. Countries that lie near the equator are warm all year long.

G

globe (glohb)
A globe is a ball with a map of the world or the earth printed on it. Globes show the size, shape, and location of continents and seas.

H

harbor (HAHR buhr)
A harbor is a place on the coast where boats can be kept in safety. Fishing boats, pleasure boats, and ships dock and refuel in a harbor.

I

Inuit (IHN yoo iht)
The Inuit are a people who live in or near the Arctic. For thousands of years the Inuit followed a special way of life adapted to their harsh environment. They hunted seals, walruses, and whales and made shelters of snow.

L

loom (loom)
A loom is a device used to weave threads into cloth. A loom can be a simple frame or an electric-powered machine.

M

map key (map kee)
A map key is a chart that shows the kinds of colors and symbols used on the map. A map tells what each color or symbol on a map stands for.

map scale (map skayl)
A map scale tells what a distance on the map equals in miles or kilometers. A map scale might tell that 1 inch (2.54 centimeters) equals 10 miles (16.09 kilometers).

mosque (mahsk)
A mosque is a building where Muslims, followers of Islam, worship. The center of religion for Muslims is the Great Mosque in Mecca, Saudi Arabia.

N

national monument (NASH uh nuhl MAHN yuh muhnt)
A national monument is a building, statue, or other thing built to remind people of a person or event important to the history of a country. The Statue of Liberty in New York, New York, and Trafalgar Square in London, England, are national monuments.

national park (NASH uh nuhl pahrk)
A national park is an area set aside by a nation's government to protect natural beauty and wildlife, such as animals, plants, mountains, and canyons. Famous national parks include Tsavo National Park in Kenya, Africa, and Great Barrier Reef in Australia.

P

papyrus (puh PY ruhs)
Papyrus is a kind of paper used in ancient times. The paper was made from the stems of the papyrus plant, a tall water plant that grows mainly in Africa. Ancient Egyptians were among the first people to use papyrus.

plains (playnz)
Plains are very large, flat areas of land. Grassy plains are sometimes called prairies.

population (PAHP yuh LAY shuhn)
A population is all of the people who live in a certain area.

preserve (prih ZURV)
A preserve is an area of land or water that is set aside to protect plants, animals, or other resources.

S

siesta (see EHS tuh)
A siesta is a nap or a period of rest after a midday meal. In many countries it is the custom for people to take a siesta every day.

souvenir (SOO vuh NIHR)
A souvenir is something that people keep to remind them of a person, place, or event. Souvenirs may be postcards, menus, ticket stubs, or photographs.

strait (strayt)
A strait is a narrow waterway that connects two larger bodies of water. The Mediterranean Sea and the Atlantic Ocean are joined by a strait.

symbol (SIHM buhl)
A symbol is an object, shape, or color that stands for or suggests another thing. On a map, a blue wavy line is often the symbol for a river.

synagogue (SIHN uh gawg)
A synagogue is a building where Jews worship and study their religion. There are many synagogues throughout the world.

T

temple (TEHM puhl)
A temple is a building people use to worship a god or gods.

terrain (tuh RAYN)
Terrain is another word for land. Special maps called terrain maps show what the surface of the land looks like.

transportation (TRANS puhr TAY shuhn)
Transportation is a way of carrying people or things from one place to another. People use bicycles, cars, trains, and planes for transportation.

W

weaving (WEEV ihng)
Weaving is making cloth by passing threads over and under each other in a crisscross pattern. People often use machines called looms to weave rugs, scarves, and clothing.

Index

This index is an alphabetical list of important topics covered in this book. It will help you find information given in both words and pictures. To help you understand what an entry means, there is sometimes a helping word in parentheses, for example, **Antarctica** (continent). If there is information in both words and pictures, you will see the words *with pictures* in parentheses after the page number. If there is only a picture, you will see the word *picture* in parentheses after the page number.

Illustration Acknowledgments

The Publishers of *Childcraft* gratefully acknowledge the courtesy of the following illustrators, photographers, agencies, and organizations for illustrations in this volume. When all the illustrations for a sequence of pages are from a single source, the inclusive page numbers are given. Credits should be read from top to bottom, left to right, on their respective pages. All illustrations are the exclusive property of the publishers of *Childcraft* unless names are marked with an asterisk (*).

192